A BRASS HA
NO MAN'S LAND

BRIG.-GEN. F. P. CROZIER, 1916

# A
# BRASS HAT
## IN
# NO MAN'S LAND

by

**BRIG.-GEN.**

## F. P. CROZIER

**C.B., C.M.G., D.S.O.**

**The Naval & Military Press Ltd**

Published by

## The Naval & Military Press Ltd

Unit 10 Ridgewood Industrial Park,
Uckfield, East Sussex,
TN22 5QE England

Tel: +44 (0) 1825 749494
Fax: +44 (0) 1825 765701

www.naval-military-press.com
www.military-genealogy.com
www.militarymaproom.com

*In reprinting in facsimile from the original, any imperfections are inevitably reproduced and the quality may fall short of modern type and cartographic standards.*

# CONTENTS

# LIST OF ILLUSTRATIONS

*A humble tribute to my Fallen Comrades who 'gave us Peace' and an expression of hope that we may, as a Nation, be worthy of their Sacrifice*

# PROLOGUE

IN the year eighteen hundred and eighty-seven, when colonial troops and statesmen had come to London for the first time, in organised array, to pay homage to the Throne, on the occasion of the fiftieth anniversary of the accession of the Great Queen – VICTORIA – a small boy played on the lawn of a pleasant Hampshire home, with tin soldiers, a drum, a gun, a bugle, and in fact the whole bag of military tricks.

Not far distant lay the New Forest – the hunting ground of monarch and guerilla, battlefield of Roundheads and Cavaliers. Hurst Castle, a place where the unlucky Charles once 'rested,' could be seen in the distance, while Carisbrooke lay across the narrow water. The guns at Spithead could be heard – firing a salute. The *Victory* kept guard over the far-flung ocean communications of the Empire at Portsmouth.

Close to the youngster sat two elderly gentlemen in easy chairs, regarding with amusement the tactical dispositions of the child, for they were his grandparents. The elder of the two men had given the greater part of his life to the Empire in India, the younger had spent many a cold night in the Crimea with the 9th Foot; after which he had retired for peace and comfort to Ireland, as a Resident Magistrate, only to find that he had passed from the frying pan into the fire, for had he not to read the Riot Act at Portumna over the sad eviction of the tenants of the late Lord Clanricarde?

The one was a lineal descendant of many a sailor; for there were always Croziers in the Royal Navy. The other, a Percy, claimed descent from Harry Hotspur and certainly inherited the temperament which had earned his *soubriquet* for that son of the House of Northumberland. This grandparent was indeed a Percy by birth, name, and nature.

While the two old men sat basking in the sun, a younger man appeared on the scene. He too was a soldier who had arrived from Burma with a Jubilee presentation, from the women of that country for the Great White Queen. Incidentally he was the youngster's father, as could easily be seen – not only in the likeness of feature – but in the way he took the child affectionately on his back for a scamper round the garden. While the romp was in progress three young men, uncles of the youngster on the Percy side, strode manfully across the grass to salute the elder generation. They too were soldiers. One, like his father, in the 9th, was about to see service in Burma; the other, a red marine, had been on constant guard in the Near East 'so that the Russians should not reach Constantinople'; while the third and youngest, a Cape mounted rifleman, had been helping to secure the Flag at the Cape.

It was a manly gathering and typically representative of two houses which had given of their best for England since long before Henry V secured the Kingdom of France at Agincourt, and had fought on almost every big battlefield in the world on which England's honour had been entrusted to English arms.

The talk must have turned to the Russian menace to India and Constantinople, for the two grandfathers definitely decided in their minds that their sons would soon be 'in the fray.'

The two older men were quite unlike each other, save in one respect – sacrifice for the Crown, and for that there was no limit. Crozier, the elder, was a highminded man of noble endeavour and spiritual inclination, and it is recorded that on this occasion he gave vent to the following peroration: – 'As we see it now there is no end to war which I, as an administrator, know to be destructive of all good and productive of little save misery. You,' he went on to say, pointing to the younger soldiers present, 'will be called upon, no doubt, to take part in much slaughter on the field of honour, and even that child there will some day play with human soldiers instead of tin ones. But, with it all, the world as I see it will one day wake up to the fact that, to quote Shakespeare, "Peace is a conquest." That will not be achieved till material factors are subordinated to moral and spiritual requirements; but it will surely come. I *know* this from the results of missionary work in India, in which, as you know, both during my service, and even more so since my retirement, I have taken the greatest possible interest.' The old man was right. In twelve years' time the child was fighting in South Africa and continued to fight almost incessantly until 1921. Perhaps the reader may have guessed that the youngster who was playing with tin soldiers on the peaceful Hampshire lawn in the Queen's Jubilee year was none other than the writer. But if the solid old grandfather was right in the one conjecture is it not within the realm of reason and reality that he should also be right in the other?

Is permanent World Peace perhaps even now in sight?

# CHAPTER I

## 1914

IT is August. The sky is clear, with not a cloud to be seen. The world war is on us, mobilisation has begun. The Atlantic rolls on to the rugged rocks of Antrim as it has always done, despite the pending upheaval and the worried thoughts in the minds of men and women. We motor swiftly along the savage coast – three friends and myself, of whom I alone am to come unscathed through the furnace. We talk and laugh and joke, each no doubt wondering how long it is to be before he is to get to grips with the enemy. As we approach Belfast there are ominous signs of war, and we are glad. To us the relief is truly great.

There have been obvious signs of civil strife during the last few months. We of Carson's army have been the victims of an ill-defined objective. Was it to be Dublin Castle, a battle against British soldiers, or nationalist Irishmen, or a bit of both? Who could tell? Who could guess? We were merely hired mercenaries, paid to do as we were bid.

Moreover we all four were, or had been, associated with the British Army, which did not make things easier. Now all is changed within a flash. Ireland is united against a common foe. Our task is manifest, our duty clear. '*Allons*,' is our cry

We reach the Ulster Club and therein see strange things. I am to see many unaccustomed sights during the next few days, but Ireland was ever the land of the unexpected, and despite its politics, nothing can take Belfast out of the Emerald Isle – save another deluge.

In the little room on the ground floor of the Ulster Club – that holy of holies – big, muscular, horsy men sit and sip and smoke, in the uniform of the North Irish Horse. Their blood is up and they are proud. Why not? Are they not to accompany the British Expeditionary Force to France? They are not regular soldiers – though many of them have been – yet they are chosen, on account of merit, to accompany the greatest, hardest, best trained, most gentlemanly little army the world has ever seen, on the greatest adventure the world has ever known. Truly they have reason to be proud! Some talk sense, some nonsense, others say nothing at all. But they all appear to think that those who get through will eat their Christmas dinners in Berlin! A few have had experience of war, though none of them knows anything of modern combat. They talk of a picnic. They think they have the responsibility of Empire on their shoulders. That is a just thought and a true. In such circumstances of national emergency, the acts and actions of each one of us reacts on the greater whole. To such is the greatness of England due. So I think as I ponder and listen to this conversation, wondering when my turn will come. My thoughts go back to nocturnal talks on the captain's deck of a German liner in the tropics, with the captain of the ship – a reserve officer of the German Imperial Navy, five years ago. 'You and I will shortly fight, my friend,' he used to say. 'There are my orders,' pointing to a safe in his cabin, 'but let it be a battle of gentlemen!' Shortly he is to be captured. Or to the inevitable breakfast salutation of Lord Charles Beresford, R.N., since 1911: 'Good-morning, all; one day nearer to the German war!' Both these sea dogs knew. Did England know? Was England told?

The gay careless fox-hunters of the north finish their drinks with a clink of glasses and rise to depart to their horses and ships, and as they do so a waiter hands me a letter on a salver. As usual in such cases, I carefully and curiously examine the back of the envelope, instead of at once opening it, to find out from whence it came! All eyes are on me, for the cover is oblong in shape and official in character. There is a silence. I read, put the letter in my pocket, and lean back in my chair.

'Coming with us?' asks one sportsman.

'No,' I reply, 'not yet. I am to join the Royal Irish Fusiliers in Dublin, and raise a company.'

This announcement is received with a roar of laughter by the departing horse soldiers as they leave the room.

'Hope your company will be well trained, Cro,' says one, Stuart by name, 'by the time we get back! You'll have to hurry up!'

'Damned young ass,' I mutter to myself, 'you don't know what you're in for, and perhaps it's just as well.'

I go to search out Captain James Craig. I may here mention, for the information of the reader, that I was, in 1914, what is called 'well placed' for war. I had served for years in the army but was yet a free-lance. That fact gave me great power of initiative; it rendered me unafraid of my superiors; it innoculated me against the fatal malady known as 'counting the personal loss'; and enabled me to take legitimate risks without fear of the future. Moreover I had served in the South African War and frontier fights, and for many years had trained my own fighting machine for my own personal use in the Hausa States. I was up-to-date and had commanded and raised the special striking force of Carson's Army. I welcomed the Great War with confidence, knowing it was not only going to be a long-drawn-out performance, but a very bloody business – a study of the Russo-Japanese War had taught me that – hence perhaps my reason for muttering that Stuart was 'a damned young ass.' He was no more an ass than the majority of his fellow countrymen!

To revert to our story: despite the fact that I am ordered to report in Dublin for duty, I am anxious – and for this reason. For seven months, in time of anxiety, I have served with, trained and commanded a small body of men, whose fighting qualities I placed second to none, for service with the Ulster Volunteer Force, in defence of Ulster and the Union. Their troubles have been my troubles, their triumphs my triumphs, their secrets my secrets – and now, at the crisis of the Empire's history, when these very men are about to change their status from orange-blooded revolutionaries to highly respectable Royal Irish Riflemen, I am ordered to join a unit not yet in being. Hence my reason for searching out Captain James Craig, the administrator of the Ulster Revolutionary movement. I determine to make a bold bid to remain with my Shankhill Road boys, instead of reporting to Dublin. The trouble is that, although it has been decided on principle that the U.V.F. should become, if possible, an army corps of the regular army, details have not yet been arranged, neither is there an Ulster establishment on which to place me. It was rumoured that the delay was being caused by some political bargain being struck in regard to Home Rule, by Sir Edward Carson. About that I know nothing, but many hundreds of men of Tyrone, exasperated by the delay, marched to the depot and enlisted on their own, their services thus being lost to the Ulster Division which was formed a little later.

I think these men were right. Lord Kitchener had called for men for the King's service and they responded.

As is often the case when there is a friend at court, my desire to remain with my own men of West Belfast was gratified with ease; and in fact my presence in Belfast, as an officer, became imperatively necessary, owing to the absence of leaders on war-services. On my shoulders, in conjunction with Colonel Couchman, late of the Somersetshire Light Infantry, my revolutionary commander, officially too old for active service, but who was soon to command the 107th (Belfast) Brigade of the 36th (Ulster) Division, fell the onus of compiling the returns for Sir Edward Carson, in so far as the capital of Ulster was concerned, which were to demonstrate to the House of Commons and to the nation, Ulster's willingness to serve in the field.

There was difficulty in obtaining the signatures of the men to serve 'unconditionally anywhere' in a Division, not because they did not want to go, but on account of the accursed Irish question. They feared the South.

It had yet to be learnt that the future of Ireland and Ulster did not lie in the House of Commons or at Dublin Castle or the Old Town Hall, Belfast, or on the strength of smuggled arms or antipapal oaths and Orange songs but on the battlefields of France and Flanders.

As I knew what every other man who took the trouble to divest himself of politics 'for the duration' likewise knew, once the lead was given men would rush to the colours to serve unconditionally, I now plead guilty to putting many a 'yes' in the more patriotic column, in order to swell the numbers for publication! My only justification for such an act can be that when the 'fall in' actually sounded Ulster was not found wanting. The truth is that the men in the street in Ulster, at the outbreak of the war, were suffering from political paralysis of the top storey and found it difficult to set themselves free from insular and parochial associations.

The musings and murmurings of an enlightened population are interesting to study in times of abnormality, and as I wander back to the Club, after fixing my fate or star to the 'Red Hand' of fortune at the headquarters, I find great interest in listening to the conversations of the crowd.

'The whole world will be fighting,' I heard one man say. 'Not unless Carson says so,' adds another. 'If those —— Papists get going when the boys is in France,' adds a third, 'there will be as much —— hell on the Shankhill and the falls for us old ——, as any of 'em will get in purgatory and Bravo Redmond will have his belly full before we've finished with them. I have my gun in the garden yet, and there's still bullets under the pulpit.'

In the midst of my reverie regarding Carson and Redmond, I feel a tap on the shoulder and on looking round come face to face with a very nice boy we call 'Bunny,' because he looks it. He too is anxious. He is employed in an office. His people will let him go to the war at once. He is young. He does not wish to run the chance of missing the war altogether! Is the Division never to be formed? If it is will it be too late? What do I advise? Shall he go to England and enlist? Kitchener wants a hundred thousand men as it is. 'Yes, Bunny,' I reply, 'Lord K. does, but he is not worrying so much about the first as about the last hundred thousand! Take my advice,' I say, 'wait: become an officer and lead your own men of North Belfast to glory.' He did. We shall hear more of Bunny later, as he died gloriously, like a man.

I turn in early to bed at my hotel. A night's rest is now more easily procured, strange to say, since the outbreak of the European War. Ireland is at peace within her boundaries. There is no necessity to sleep with loaded six-shooter under pillow now, nor to lock and bolt the bedroom door, piling furniture against it in addition, lest some masked counter-revolutionary or burglar taking full advantage of the domestic chaos should desire to have a word with me at the revolver's mouth. All these possibilities I am spared in view of the greater danger over the water; yet, for four months previously, I had put up with and accepted the desperate situation. Few in Belfast slept as I slept in those days, surrounded by armed guards, land mines, electric alarms as well as stacks of valuable ammunition worth their weight in gold, smuggled to me through the customs, disguised as butter, thanks to the infidelity of an official, who had temporarily forgotten his trust, or stands of arms from Germany, the country with which we are now actually at war! All that is over. I can now sleep without fear of assassination by a fellow countryman.

It does not often fall to the lot of an officer on the active list to take part in ceremonial of a friendly nature with the King's troops and troops of a quasi-revolutionary tinge, yet such was to be my good luck. It so happens that I have long family connections with the Norfolk Regiment, a battalion of which was to embark with the 15th Infantry Brigade, under Brigadier-General Count Gleichen, at Belfast for the front. I was therefore pleased when I was asked to arrange the ceremony for the handing over of the colours of the 'Holy boys,' to the custody of the authorities of Belfast cathedral for safe keeping during the absence of the battalion on service. It was not only a peculiar function; but, I should think, one quite unique in the annals of the British army. A detachment of the 1st Norfolk Regiment was present of course, with colours and colour-party, while a guard of honour of Revolutionary troops of Carson's army, drawn from the West Belfast Regiment, with their colours, presented arms with German Mauser rifles, which had been smuggled in, during the gun-running episode of a few months previously, under the nose of the British fleet which, we were told, had put the blind eye to the telescope. Was there ever such confusion! Five months previously these very men of the Norfolks had quitted Belfast for Holyrood, owing to the menace in their midst of the very men who were doing them honour now, and from whom they evidently felt disposed to accept the compliment. Soon they were to fight shoulder to shoulder in France.

At last the day arrives for the silent secret departure of the 15th Infantry Brigade for a destination unknown but easily surmised.

It is a Sunday. I repair with others to the Royal Ulster Yacht Club at Bangor for lunch, and subsequently, from the luxury of the lounge, view with greedy eyes the majestic passage of the convoy of escorted transports laden with their precious human freight, which was to make history by valour, tenacity and sharp-shooting, in a few days time at Elouges and elsewhere. Our time was not yet!

During the succeeding weeks I am busy, my chief task being to keep Carson's irregulars out of mischief. I have a narrow escape at night on return to the armoury where I sleep. One of my own men, a good fellow when sober, a dangerous fool in drink, decides by the aid of Guinness – a popular beverage on the Shankhill – that he has a grievance against me, I having previously spoken to him about his abnormal consumption of alcoholic beverages of all kinds, and its danger to himself and his neighbours. Exactly what happened I am at a loss to know, but the result is with me still in the shape of a bump behind the ear! My guard, I am told, picked me up and looked after me while Grant, my assailant, still full of Guinness and grievous ardour, took up a strategic position in the doorway of his house, which was directly opposite the entrance to my temporary stronghold, with a loaded rifle and five rounds of ammunition daring anybody to come out! When

I am myself again, I am made acquainted with the situation. As our rooms are dim, it being not unnaturally surmised that a lighted candle would prove too much for our hilarious brigand opposite, I peer through a window into the dark only to behold our friend ready and expectant. We turn in and leave him to it, till sleep and thirst, sharpened by impatience, get the better of him.

In the morning I sauntered over to Grant's house, with bandaged head, to be informed that he is not very well, and is in fact confined to bed. I go up to see him. He remembers nothing of the night before, and is quite polite and docile till I take up the rifle and ammunition beside his bed, and hand them to an orderly. Then the scene is changed to fury. Had not Carson given him the rifle? Had not Carson said on parade that no man was to take it from him? Grant put up a good fight, but there is safety in numbers, and he got the hammering of his life and two thick ears. It was thought that this lesson would have been enough, but, alas, the drink had too firm a hold, and, after he had expended much patience and ingenuity in gaining entry to my abode on several subsequent occasions, I was forced to crave the support of the A.P.M., who wheeled him up in front of the magistrate.

A discussion behind closed doors between Mr. Nagle, Colonel Hill-Trevor and myself leads to a promise of reform and a pledge to enlist in my battalion when once recruiting for the Ulster Division starts, the court being cleared in order that publicity should not be given to this disgraceful performance, attributable, no doubt, to the stupid man himself but also to the drink he had been taking. The pleasant sequel to this incident is yet to come. Grant did not go to the war, being too old; but he served under me as a sergeant faithfully and well till our time came to go down to the sea in ships, and subsequently carried on the torch of sobriety and all that goes with it, in a reserve battalion, till the cease-fire sounded. He never looked back again.

Stories in the meantime keep drifting back to Ulster from France, through the mouths of wounded men, and I have great difficulty in restraining the most war-loving, and therefore the most valuable of my West Belfasters from joining up at Victoria Barracks. The great feats of valour of the Irish Regiments on the field of honour do more to stimulate martial desire than any recruiting orator or poster could hope to do. It is history repeating itself. Colenso and the Tugela, Ladysmith and its relief are still fresh in our minds only fourteen years ago.

'What *are* these politicians doing?' I hear on every side! Ulster is rising from her orange-coloured gas attack at last, and is beginning to see red. Lord Kitchener never understood Ireland, I am told. Why should he have done so? There is a degree of difference between the fellaheen of Egypt and peasants of Antrim and Connemara!

One morning in September *my* eyes see red – not metaphorically speaking, but in reality. The cause? Brass hats! The locality is sombre enough in all conscience, as the hospitable Ulster Club can never be mistaken for a Hall of Laughter. I jump to it that at long last the Ulster men are to become respectable soldiers and that these staff officers are among us for the purpose of transformation. The senior, a Colonel, Tom Hickman, M.P. for Wolverhampton and hero of many fights under Lord K., is kindly and well-disposed towards us, and, above all, is 'in with the clique' at the War Office – which is all to the good. The other, more junior and of the reserve from Dublin, represents 'Q' of the Irish command. He too is well-disposed and helpful and has, as his primary task, the quartering of the new division and the erection of vast camps of corrugated iron. But the fates are against him. It is discovered in the Ulster Club (how, goodness only knows), that the man from Dublin is a papist! A hurried line to an influential General in England and he disappears in a fog of secrecy almost as quickly as he came! Catholicism may be all right to be allied with in

France. Lutheranism may be all right within the hostile ranks of the German army; but no papist shall put huts up for Ulster men in Ulster!'

My luck is in. I am told to proceed to London, there to see Charles Craig, M.P., a first-class natural soldier, brother of James of Craigavon, who has made some arrangements about the recruiting of sergeant-instructors at Whitehall. I have not been in England since 1913. Now I see a nation in arms at its very best.

Being in uniform I am given free drives in trains, trams and buses within the Metropolitan area. Two months previously, had an officer been caught in either of the latter in uniform, his Colonel would possibly have called upon him to resign his commission!

My work is to send over to Belfast, daily, as many ex-N.C.O.'s as I can, in order that the training may be expedited. Lord K. has called upon the ex-non-commissioned warriors of the past, the backbone of the armies of Egypt, the Sudan, South Africa, the Indian Frontier and China, to become once more the backbone of England's newest and mightiest force, the national army of the salt of the earth. It has been confidently said that on the Day of Judgment a British N.C.O. will probably be found imploring his neighbours not to get the wind up. The British N.C.O. is never wanting in time of danger, whether it be in shielding his battalion, colonel, captain or subaltern from the too inquisitive enquiries of some tiresome general or 'knowall' staff-officer, or in placing his body between the enemy and his country. He is always ready. He is always on the spot. When Lord K. asked the 'backbone' of the past to come forward, in their old ranks, and as far as possible, their old corps, to help him and the eager youngsters who were clamouring to fight, he knew his appeal would not fall on deaf ears. He was, as usual, right.

My instructions are to go to the Horse-Guards parade daily at 3 p.m. and to choose from the stalwarts lined up on the grounds upon which the King reviews his Guards, as many men as I can, and dispatch them to Ulster by the mail train each night. It has been my good fortune to see many fine inspiring military pageants in my time. Colonial troops passing before the venerable Queen in 1897 filled me with pride; steady deployment under withering rifle fire during the relief of Ladysmith made me realise what the British regular soldier was; but never before had I set eyes on a more magnificent military spectacle than on the day I walked through the arch from the War Office to choose from the pick of the 'backbone.' These men were in mufti, some were toffs and some wore mufflers, some had obviously grown prosperous in civil life, others, it was easy to see, had endured the struggle so often imposed on fighting men, when once the danger is over and they are forgotten on their return to civil life. Now, on this September afternoon, they stand erect, some with medals, many without – there never was a time when a pawnshop would not give a few pence to a starving stalwart for his 'left breast gongs' – steady and still – the same outward signs of discipline. They are of all ages, from perhaps thirty-five to sixty-five. Those over sixty say they are forty, and if necessary hide their tell-tale medals. Those who must, lose their discharge papers, while the only thing that matters now is to 'get there' – as it was in the days of old. Into this conspiracy against *Anno Domini* I enter with glee. I realise that if a youth of sixteen is justified (as he is) in swearing he is eighteen in order to serve his country, the veteran of fifty-five is even more justified in saying he is less in order to be able to teach his junior. There are some three hundred non-commissioned veterans for me to choose from, and as I walk round the ranks my eyes fall on a familiar face. The body is a little stouter, but the cheery iron look is just the same.

'Gorring!' I exclaim. His face lights up. 'Come with me?' I ask.

'Anywhere, sir,' is the only reply, and not a muscle moves.

31

Gorring had been my orderly-room sergeant and colour-sergeant in the Nigerian Mounted Infantry, ten years previously. A cheery fellow, of the Royal Berkshire Regiment, he had served in Mounted Infantry in the South African War and against Fulani rebels in the Hausa States and sang a very good song at smoking concerts, when once warmed up, his *chef-d'œuvre* being a ditty entitled: 'By studying economy, I live like a lord.'

'All right,' I reply, 'but you must study economy!' At which remark the slightest of slight smiles becomes visible at the corners of the lips. After the parade I tell Gorring to go round to my room at the Victoria Hotel, quite handy. I order drinks, Gorring had a whisky and soda, and I a ginger ale. 'Here's to speedy promotion, sir,' says the old warrior – incapable of taking advantage – 'but I'm surprised to see you drinking ginger ale, sir.'

'Well, you see, Gorring,' I say, 'I'm studying economy! Moreover, in this war, for what I shall have to do, I can never do it on whisky. Things are more serious now than they were at Zaria, when Colonel Cubitt used to sing "Sally in our Alley" to us at 3 a.m. and be on parade at 6. West Africa plus cocktails nearly killed me, and I gave up all drink several years ago.'

As my old friend lives in London I attest him, to give him pay and allowances of his old rank, and keep him back to supervise the daily draft to Ulster. It is always so in the army. What should we do without our 'backbone.'

I have said that I stayed at the Victoria Hotel, for convenience. During my few weeks there, I was pestered in the smoking-room by all sorts and conditions of business men, who had got to know of my connection with the Ulster Division and who were not out for 'business as usual,' which was the misguided slogan of the period, unless the pre-war meaning of that term meant the giving of vast bribes for orders! Profiteering began early.

At last my quota of N.C.O.'s is complete, and I return to Belfast by way of Glasgow, where it falls to my lot to collect a draft of several hundreds of Glasgow Orangemen, who had expressed a desire to serve in the Division under the red hand of Ulster. I can draw a veil over the scenes at the Clydeside city, and at Ardrossan, save to say that a more drunken orgy I have never witnessed. Bands, banners, booze and blasphemy run riot. At last the ship is reached and with it safety, for a merchant captain has power at sea and a hose pipe! The orange lions become sober lambs. Sad is the sight when I march them to Victoria Barracks in the morning, heads aching, throats ablaze and not a hope of beer till the opening of the canteen in six hours time! Old Gorring thought it one of the toughest jobs he had ever had, which says a lot.

I find, on arrival, that the Belfast brigade of the Ulster Division is complete. My West Belfast irregulars have become the 9th battalion Royal Irish Rifles. They are destined to carry the banner and high record of the regiment to the very summit of unselfish self-sacrifice and service in less than a year's time on the battlefields of France and Flanders.

I find that I am promoted major, second-in-command, from the Royal Irish Fusiliers, which I never joined, and that my new commanding officer is Lieutenant-Colonel G. S. Ormerod, late of the Munsters. My new C.O. and I lunch together, in mufti, into which I change, while a handy tailor alters my badges of rank. I tell my Colonel all about his new command and take stock of him as I talk. He is a wonderful man. Aged just over sixty, he served in Burma and South Africa with the Munsters, for which campaigns he holds the medals. Retired for age, as a major, after long service in the East, he commanded a special reserve battalion of his regiment for more than the allotted span. Now, once more, he comes forward to fill the breach, active, fit and alert in body and mind, at a time of life when many men are in retirement, the reward of an ordered and reasonable existence. A great cricketer and sportsman, Colonel Ormerod belongs to the M.C.C. and bats regularly at the nets at

Lord's. There is a difference of twenty-five years in age between us; he being old enough, in the familiar phrase, to be my father. But we shall get on together.

After lunch we drive down to Newcastle on the coast of Down by the mountains of Mourne, and find our battalion under canvas at Donard Lodge, in company with the men of South Belfast, now the 10th Royal Irish Rifles. The command of this battalion has been given to a warrior of the Indian Army, Colonel Bernard, a cousin of the Archbishop of Dublin. The officers of the two battalions mess together in the Lodge. The position of Camp Commandant is held by Colonel Bob Wallace, Grand Master of the Orange Lodges, who commanded the South Down Militia during the South African War, receiving a C.B. for his services. We are a happy party. Colonel Bernard has for his second-in-command Major John Bernard, who had been my military mentor and teacher in the old 4th Middlesex V.R.C. (now 13th Kensingtons) of which Corps he was adjutant before the South African War.

Our meeting at mess is cordial. Far away at Ballykinlar the remaining two battalions of the brigade are quartered. We realise there is little time left of autumn for training, for it is now October. We are a ragtailed crowd. However, by degrees, we obtain clothing – the Ulster Volunteer organisation

35

sold boots and khaki to the War Office! – and conquer the rudiments of platoon and company drill,
under the shadow of Slieve Donard, in the beautiful
park of the young Lord Annesley who gave his life
for country in the early days. Soon the wintry
weather drives us into billets, but before Christmas
is upon us we are ensconced in a tin camp of our
own at Ballykinlar, with the 10th Rifles alongside
us and 8th and 15th not far off.

It is not possible to raise a regiment or battalion
in billets with any degree of satisfaction or hope of
efficiency. The barrack rooms and the officers' and
sergeants' messes are the places where discipline is
forged and character moulded. Till now, we have
been only existing, but with new quarters, we start
to live.

It is no easy task to knock a thousand men into
orderly shape with only the help of ex-non-commissioned officers, themselves in need of refreshing, and
thirty officers of low rank – second lieutenants – all
on the square and quite devoid of military knowledge. Yet this is being done, and for it the credit
is largely due to one Membry – now Captain and
Adjutant – an old colour-sergeant of the line.
Membry had no war service, which was not his
fault; but he knew his drill, he knew the routine of
orderly room and regiment and he 'knew the ropes'
as few whom I have ever met.

The task of Membry is no easy one! The subalterns are wild. He sets himself to giving them hell on the quiet and well he does it. Even the boys will now admit he succeeded very well, and made them efficient officers, able to hold their own in any military situation. They were head and shoulders over average war-time Napoleons, thanks to Membry.

We (the Colonel and I) concentrate on two things at the outset; knocking the beer and politics out of all ranks and building up *esprit-de-corps* in its place on the one hand, while on the other we foster, inculcate, teach and build up the blood lust for the discomfiture of the enemy, without which no war is possible – for long – and no victory certain, for 'the great game' is now a pose, and its chief bulwark is propagandic suggestion.

By deportment and example in the mess the Colonel works wonders without saying a word. The drink bill lessens. In the orderly room the 'drunk or sober' question remains acute for some time, but discipline in the canteen has its own reward.

Before Christmas the Colonel asks me to undertake the tactical training of the officers for war, from the theoretical point of view, by means of lectures after mess. It is agreed that I lecture nightly from Monday to Friday. This I do for six months. My first lecture, notes of which I have before me, ran on these lines :—

'Gentlemen, the Commanding Officer has asked me to undertake your training for war, by nightly lectures. I shall try to make you interested. I shall run through Field Service Regulations, Parts 1 and 2, Infantry training, combined training, a little topography, organisation and equipment, military law and certain campaigns of history. I shall not stress the present war. All wars are much the same, the details merely vary, owing to climate, geography, numbers engaged and equality or inequality of forces. We can teach you to form fours, drill, put out outposts, advance, flank and rear guards and the whole bag of tricks, in a short time. Any fool can do these things. They must be learnt but they are only the beginning. I can teach you the offensive spirit to a certain extent – I have it myself – but it is largely born in a man, not made. The all-important thing for you to learn is intellectual discipline. Let me give you an example or two. In this battalion the wish expressed by the C.O. is tantamount to an order – no matter what it may be. He won't let you down. Moreover, if the C.O. says a thing is black, it's black, no matter if it appears white to you. In other words, don't argue. Now, during the South African War an action was fought at Spion Kop, a big hill or mountain. They were told by superior authority to take *and hold* Spion Kop. They took it without loss. *They didn't hold it.* Had they done so they would have relieved Ladysmith and saved the lives of men and women starving and dying of sickness. They retreated. They abandoned the hill. Never retreat. Never abandon unless you are told to. The responsible officer on Spion Kop was not told to retreat. There was an utter lack of intellectual discipline. The excuses given for the *débâcle*, one can call it nothing else, were futile and ill-advised. These reasons for retreat were: lack of ammunition, lack of food, water, artillery support, as well as too much enemy shell fire which apparently could not be helped. Never have to give any excuse for retiring – don't retire unless you're ordered to. Contrast the action of General Smith-Dorrien, a few months ago at Le Cateau, with the abandonment of Spion Kop. The General said last August: "when men are too tired to march, they must lie down and fight." There's nothing else left to do. That first principle has been acted on by thousands of British soldiers in the past and in the last three or four months in France in particular. But it isn't as easy as it looks apparently. The poor senior fellows on Spion Kop hadn't evidently learnt it during many years' service. You must drill yourselves to obey this first principle subconsciously even when you are weary, hungry, thirsty, frightened or "fed up."

'Closely allied to this principle and an important

part of your intellectual discipline, is your conquest of fear. All soldiers – except the most dense and unintelligent – are frightened in action, at times. There comes that pain in the tummy. That you have to master. You must never let your neighbour know you are in a funk, either by word, deed or suggestion. Funk itself is nothing. When unchained it becomes a military menace, and for that men die at the hands of their comrades. Much of my talks will be upon matters not directly found in military books.

'You must lose your gentle selves. You must steel your hearts and minds to be callous of life or death. That is war.'

\*    \*    \*    \*

The memorable year of 1914 closes with the hope that we shall soon be 'in it.'

We have the usual Christmas dinners, leave, festivities and rejoicing. I go to London for ten days and become a civilian in mufti.

I find the ladies are very pressing in the metropolis, with white feathers for men unwilling to fight. Going to the Alhambra to book seats I meet one in Coventry Street. She presents her feather and smiles. I do likewise.

'Why are you not in uniform?' she asks. 'Afraid to fight?' And so on. 'A visit to the recruiting officer?' she suggests.

'Certainly, if you wish,' I reply.

Off we toddle together to Trafalgar Square. The recruiting officer smiles at Miss Busybody and looks at me.

'A bit on the short side! However, times are hard !' he says condescendingly.

Many questions are asked me. 'Well, I haven't actually served before, I am serving,' I state.

'What the hell are you doing here then?' asks the great man.

'I don't know, I'm sure. Better ask the lady,' I reply.

Both look blankly at each other and then at me.

'Who are you, what are you?' she asks.

'A Major in the Royal Irish Rifles,' I reply.

I hope, if she is alive to-day, this well-meaning and patriotic lady will work as hard in the cause of Peace as she did in the cause of War. She may, if she completes the patriotic circle, find opportunity of making fewer mistakes!

# CHAPTER II

## MOULDING THE MACHINE

THE first half of 1915 is spent by us in perfecting our military machine for war. Colonel Ormerod creates detailed regularity by means of precise and exacting kit inspections which he holds weekly; and by the frequent unexpected and somewhat informal supervision of barracks. Our heaven-sent friend, the Quartermaster, Capt. Jim Newton, a king among kings in his own specific line, does more than most to inculcate the military method into the everyday affairs of life. I, for my part, do what I can to alter completely the outlook, bearing, and mentality of over a thousand men in as short a time as possible – for blood-lust is taught for purposes of war in bayonet-fighting itself and by doping the minds of all with propagandic poison. The German atrocities (many of which I doubt in secret), the employment of gas in action, the violation of French women, and the 'official murder' of Nurse Cavell all help to bring out the brute-like bestiality which is so necessary for victory. The process of 'seeing red,' which has to be carefully cultured if the effect is to be lasting, is elaborately grafted into the make-up of even the meek and mild, through the instrumentality of martial music, drums, Irish pipes, bands and marching songs. Sacred and artistic music is forbidden, save at Church, and even then the note of combat is struck. The Christian Churches are the finest blood-lust creators which we have and of them we made free use.

The British soldier is a kindly fellow and it is safe to say, despite the dope, seldom oversteps the mark of barbaric propriety in France, save occasionally to kill prisoners he cannot be bothered to escort back to his lines.

In order that he shall enter into the true spirit of the show however, the fun of the fair as we may call it, it is necessary to corrode his mentality with bitter-sweet vice and to keep him up to the vicious scratch on all occasions. Casualties are never alluded to save in the vein of callous or careless regret. It is my hope that in days to come, in the near future, the men will not only regard death, gashing and gaping wounds, gas-destroyed organs, or even frozen feet (this latter a carelessly acquired condition, in most cases, and one which meets with severe retribution from the disciplinary point of view) as mere nothings, but that they will be able to joke lightly among themselves in these matters, fortified by the fact that they are giving more gashes, ripping up more bodies and causing more suffering generally than the other side. By September, 1915, everything we do is faultless, everything the Germans do is abominable. It is the only way in war, and both sides follow it.

I regard this course of suggestion as a means to an end. I myself can adopt the pose at will. I do not really hate the Germans – I say I do. I really do not like to 'see the red blood flow,' but there are men who will swear to this day that I revel in it, and like nothing better! I know that 'blood-lust' and 'the offensive spirit', 'callous disregard for casualties,' 'domination' are all allied. Secretly, I have great regard for casualties, but now only because loss weakens our strength. I grudge an unnecessary life lost on patrol or during a raid, merely because it means one soldier less; but I think nothing of 'throwing away' (so said the ignorant) a thousand men in half an hour, provided a position is gained or held; but on the other hand, I think nothing of sending a colonel about his business, because he allows his men to be unnecessarily subjected to avoidable bombardment, or really 'throws away' valuable lives on a position *lost* or a trench *untaken*. This is my war creed – my pose.

The all-important matter – the conquering of personal fear – I find is best dealt with by means of lectures on *esprit-de-corps*, regimental history, stories of the great military achievements of past wars and the personal sacrifices in France and Flanders in 1914 and 1915 – by our wonderful men of all classes – even unto death. A single instance will illustrate this pride of regiment. Someone – I know not who – devised a Divisional cap badge, comprising the Red Hand of Ulster, to be worn by the whole of the Ulster Division. The political suggestion was approved by the higher authorities, without our knowledge. The badges arrived, were issued, and of course worn, since an order is an order; but regimental tradition prevailed over political stupidity. Protests reached Divisional Headquarters in such large numbers, in the regulation manner, that within a week the Royal Irish Rifles badge was again in every cap. It is possible to play on regimental tradition to almost any extent, provided the way is known, but it cannot be cut across for apparently no good military reason.

No army is ever a hundred per cent. perfect in the matter of 'blood-lust' or 'offensive spirit.' The personal factor alone prevents this. There are in all armies men who seek safety and angle for jobs behind the lines and even at home. The high ideal to be aimed at is that every officer goes to a base or soft staff appointment under protest, as his heart is in the firing line. Despite the high quality of our wonderful Expeditionary Force which achieved almost the impossible in 1914 and 1915 there were officers, some quite fit, some a little sick, and some a little tired, who sought shelter in safety on the very first opportunity and remained 'dug in' until the last shot was fired. To say this is not to cast any slur on the wonderful men of 1914, but to illustrate my difficulty in 1915. I have to produce, if possible, a set of regimental officers who, although they have never been soldiers before, will not desire to slink off to home jobs if they find themselves at home sick or wounded, or in other ways able to do so. I have to produce men and mere boys, on arrival in France, who will stick anything and stick at nothing to achieve victory. The officers who went out to France with the battalion in 1915 almost answered the hundred per cent. test. Some fell by the wayside, it is true; but only a very few showed any desire whatever to quit the war zone or the firing line for a safer and more comfortable appointment. In fact, it is safe to say that none wished to be anywhere else than in the firing line with the battalion, despite the fact that a few, being temperamentally unfitted for war and a danger to our side, failed. Colonel Ormerod's personal example contributed largely to this high standard of moral efficiency of the officers of his battalion. He was over sixty years of age and no one dared say him nay: how then could the

LIEUT.-COLONEL G. S. ORMEROD AND OFFICERS, 9TH ROYAL IRISH RIFLES, 1915

youngsters show the white feather? The question of the temperamental fitness of soldiers to be ordered into the line and shot if they fail to stay there was one which, of course, I could not discuss with my own officers in the training stage. My duty was to teach them the Regulations and the Army Act where they could see the penalties, and to help them to overcome the difficulties which impel to desertion, cowardice and such-like offences which, in their case, if indulged in, lead to trouble and even death by shooting at the hands of comrades. The question of ability to 'stick it' or to do the right thing in the right way, in action, is largely one of morale; but the fact cannot be overlooked that fear of the consequences undoubtedly plays an important part in the reasoning powers of men distracted by fear, cold, hunger, thirst or complete loss of morale and staying power. I should be very sorry to command the finest army in the world on active service without the power behind me which the fear of execution brings. Those who wish to abolish the death sentence for cowardice and desertion in war should aim at a higher mark and strive to abolish war itself. The one is the product of the other. Some people, particularly Labour Cabinet ministers and leaders seem to think that 'fear' itself is a crime in war. Fear is no more a crime in war than in peace. Inability to control or smother fear is an unpardonable and dangerous crime in war and, as it is contagious, must be treated like any other disease in peace time – abolished. I would remind the advocates of the abolition of the death sentence in war that to catch an infectious disease in peace time is no crime; but to foster its spread, by non-notification is an offence against society which is rightly punished.

The sex question played a large part in my training syllabus both of officers and men. By June, 1915, we were away from Ireland. The water divided the married men from their wives, in the case of the private soldiers and non-commissioned officers. The young officers, mostly under twenty years of age, were for the first time in their lives far from the influence of home. Brighton was close. In the case of the officers, London, Brighton, Eastbourne and other resorts offered inducements of which the uninitiated boys of Belfast had seldom heard, let alone experienced. The times were abnormal. Who could tell, might they not all be 'pushing up the daisies' in some foreign field shortly? Why not have a fling and enjoy the pleasures of sexual intercourse while the chance was there? As for the men – the other ranks – it is a fact that prostitutes and loose women always follow the big drum. The more big drums there are the more prostitutes abound. There were a lot of drums in England and France in 1915.

Unfortunately many of the boys were new to the big drums. Of course I regarded the matter entirely from the point of view of efficiency and casualties. There was not much good teaching men to be good soldiers, if the prostitutes or highly placed amateurs frustrated our efforts. My attention was first called to the trouble by the entry of a very efficient young officer into a private hospital where an operation was performed. He was only eighteen years of age. At first I thought he had fallen a victim to venereal disease, but on making enquiries I found out he had submitted to an operation because he had injured himself while indulging himself for the first time, at a high-class brothel which was conducted on very select and exclusive lines at a private house. I had a long chat with the boy, as by this time most of the troubles used to be brought to me, in preference to the Colonel, as they knew me better and I was more of their age. 'Well Sir,' he said quite frankly, 'I don't want to get laid up in France, I am going there to fight, and if I did not have it done I would damage myself again!' I elicited from my young friend that he had been with others to a certain place where innocents and hardened sinners were provided for the accommodation of the chaste and the defiled. Of course this did not astound me, as I know war. I had been in Cape Town and Durban during the South African picnic, and I knew such things always went on, wherever large bodies of troops congregate for war. One had become accustomed to that sort of thing in other countries on a large scale but, in our England, somehow, the idea didn't go down quite so smoothly. In 1914 England changed her soul, otherwise she would have lost. I was able, by arrangement with a medical officer, to ensure that every officer, N.C.O. and rifleman was instructed and had access to disinfectants after indulgence in sexual intercourse, and that many of the girls and women had opportunities afforded them of similar facilities, free of charge. Through these means we were able to congratulate ourselves, on embarkation for France in the latter quarter of 1915, that although we had not yet had opportunity of distinguishing ourselves in the Field, our discretion in the boudoir had been admirable!

Some may say that in making arrangements for the limitation of venereal disease in this manner I was condoning or even encouraging vice. I appreciate their point of view; but I would remind them we were at war, fighting for our lives, and that war breeds vice and venereal. One is the corollary of the other. The abnormal life, the shattered nerves, the longing to forget, if even for one brief moment, the absence from home and the inculcation of barbaric habits in our manhood, tempered by the most beautiful acts of heroism, unselfishness, sacrifice to duty, even unto death, lead directly and inevitably to the path of free love on a large, elaborate and ever-expanding scale. My job was to provide food for cannon and good food at that. Far better to eradicate the cause – war itself – than to build up false hopes that it can be waged in any other way than by brute force and brutal means. I go so far as to say that free love in discretion for many of the celibates of both sexes, engaged in war work between 1914 and 1918, was as inevitable as the rising and the setting of the sun.

The day of parting in war is, to married men at least, the darkest day of all. It is a day to which no modern wife or mother should be again subjected. The strain is too great, the load too heavy. Men go, win glory, achieve success – or failure; it is a toss up which – keep buoyed up by excitement and ever-changing scene, or even starve in mud or slush without hope of a tot of rum or dry billet, while the women wait, long, endure in silence with aching hearts. It's not good enough. The risks are too great, the temptations too appalling. I do not write of the sheltered homes but of the homes of the multitude. The women themselves can now see to it, as they have the power, that no more women suffer as did my wife and mother on that September eve at Liphook, under the spreading chestnut tree – the old original tree of the poem –

when I passed out to the darkness and glory of gory battle, accompanied by one thousand of the flower of Ulster, few of whom returned. I see the two women now, erect, brave, British, standing at the cottage door – I wonder how many poor women stood there later under similar conditions – blowing a kiss as I pass at the head of half a battalion. Not a flinch, not a tear. I look to the left and salute – the child calls out 'Daddy!' The band starts up. That's better. 'Left . . .Left . . .Left,' shouts the sergeant-major. We pass on into the dark of night. We are now as steel, hardened to endure anything and everything for England.

When we leave Liphook, by train, for an unknown destination which turns out to be Folkestone, I have plenty of time to ruminate over the work of the last twelve months as I look at the carriage full of careless boys playing bridge and joking – fodder for cannon! And what a change has come over them since first I met them in mufti. Now they know as much about soldiering after a year's service, as it is possible for juniors to know – far more than I ever knew at their age – and the world holds no secrets from them. Would they stand the acid test – ordeal by battle? – is the question I ask myself. I feel confident in them. I trust them; and that trust was never misplaced.

# CHAPTER III

IT is a strange thing that when soldiers in war are alone together, undisturbed, they are liable to do things they would never otherwise think of doing. We cross the Channel in safety to Boulogne, in silence, without lights. No smoking is allowed. The sea is calm. It is pitch dark on deck. On arrival the Colonel finds he knows the Rest Camp commandant who comes to meet us. I fall the battalion in and march up the steep hill to where we are to spend the night or such of it as is left. Next morning the Colonel comes to me with anxious face and says there is a complaint against the battalion. During the voyage over someone had climbed through the porthole of the wine bar which was locked, and had extracted ten pounds worth of liquor! Someone had drunk it, although no bottles are to be found! 'What shall we do?' he asks. It looks as if 'we' did it; but supposing a steward had? 'Nobody was drunk,' I say; ' but we had, I think, better pay to avoid a bad mark on arrival in the country.' We pay up, and, falling the battalion in, ask if anybody knows anything about it. Of course not a man moves; so the men who were on that part of the deck nearest to the bar are placed under stoppages to make good the amount. Such is war – and 'booze.'

We are all pleased to be over the water at last and none more so than the Colonel. Grand old chap: for the last month in England he has suffered agonies lest it should be said he was too old for war! Now he is younger than ever! We stay in camp all day, as the men are not allowed to go into the town and it is our rule to do as they do, within reason. Let us look around and see what officers we have got to lead these men to victory. As all joined together about the same time, as subalterns, it is natural that age should count for promotion to Major and Captain, other things being equal. The officer problem had been difficult, as all knew too much about each other's business and there was a tendency to bring the petty rivalries of civilian life into the mess. This we have stamped out. The junior Major is P. J. Woods, who, having regard to previous active service experience in the South African War, joined as a full lieutenant in 1914. George Gaffikin, a schoolmaster in England, and a public school and varsity man of portly build, Horace Haslett, a Belfast merchant and his brother-in-law Willie

Montgomery, a Belfast surveyor and auctioneer, complete the senior list. We had introduced some English public-school element into the officer ranks, from England, in addition to some men from Liverpool whom I had run across while in the port of Lancashire on recruiting duty. One of the latter, whom we may call by his nick-name Tom Foy, is destined to become quite a celebrity in his way, in France, and we shall come across him later. The remaining captains and subalterns are a good lot.

No account of the immediately important part of the personnel of our band of merry men can be complete without reference to my batman, David Starrett, who, joining up at sixteen, became my personal help in 1914 because of his reliability. He was a total abstainer, unshackled to drink, and remained with me until 1919, by which time he had become my friend, confidant and universal provider, as well as a war veteran of the big battles of his time, before reaching the ripe age of twenty-one. McKingstry, my groom, an ex-lancer of uncertain temper, also did me well and kept his horses fit when those of others perished, until demobilised in 1919. My orderly, Hackett, a dapper little soldier of the old school, a Rifleman of many years' standing, parted company with me in the early days of our great adventures, in circumstances which will be described later.

The order comes to move and we are not sorry.
Rest Camps, on account of their ever fluctuating
populations, are uncomfortable places, save for the
permanent staff, who, if they are wise and efficient,·
rightly make themselves at home.

We train to the Vicnacourt area where we meet
our transport which has crossed to Rouen from
Southampton. I have a nice billet with a mother
and daughter, a pretty girl of some twenty summers.
The only son is in the trenches. They do me well,
and, as I lie in bed reading on the first night, the
girl, clad only in simple nightdress, brings me a hot
water bottle, unasked. Her long hair nestles round
her neck and over her shoulders. *Dormez bien!* she
laughingly and quite naturally exclaims. I, doubt-
ingly, acquiesced and put the light out. Next night
there is more water bottle and conversation. Is
Monsieur married? How many children has he?
How old are they? Is Monsieur happy? Next
morning we receive our orders to proceed by march
route to the trenches. I funk the billet! On the
principle that it is a dirty bird which fouls its own
nest, it is good that we receive marching orders
quickly, but I am yet to learn that many billets are
much the same in France. 'Why not?' they argue;
'the war is long, life is short, it cannot now be too
sweet, let it be as sweet as is possible'. This 'free
love in billets' habit is understandable – as a biolo-

gical-cum-psychological occurrence in the disorderly life of an ordered period of violent and tragic upheaval, and in itself, was fairly safe, as the women and girls were generally clean. Exactly the same thing went on, in lesser degree, during the latter part of the South African War, before the Boer families were taken from the farms and placed in concentration camps, in the absence of the men. Where the real danger arises is when the easily acquired habit of 'billet free love' becomes part and parcel of the make up of the youngsters, who, in finding themselves at the bases, on courses, going on leave or coming back to hell on earth, naturally continue to indulge in their newly found and easily acquired sexual gratifications, often alas! under less favourable and safe conditions than in the billets of the farms and villages. In the billets the girls see to it that preventatives are used, for their own dual protection and, in fact, often keep a stock of requisites for purposes of safety and profit. Not so in the towns and cities. There the women cannot keep pace with the demand, with the result that large venereal hospitals are established for officers and men in France and England, while in all classes of society at home, from the highest to the lowest, the peacetime barriers are relaxed 'for the duration.' The habits acquired in the billets of France and Flanders and in other seats of war spread rapidly to Mayfair and Whitechapel and all the places in between. I even heard a good judge of war say a man – or boy – in 1918, could not fight well unless he could love well. At the bases and in the towns, when boys are more on their own, going and coming, lounging in clubs, hotels, and *estaminets*, the danger of excessive drinking must be added to the toll, as drink excites the sexual organs and makes men careless. Such a state of affairs could never come about in normal times for lack of opportunity, if for no other reason. Given the opportunity, much is possible; but the real cause is reaction after violent action, superimposed upon opportunity. The same kind of thing began to take place during the General Strike, when both sexes were thrown together unceremoniously and with ease. In each case the methods of arbitrament were to blame, not the unfortunate or unconsulted people who became victims of their own degrading handiwork, for world war or industrial peace is a personal responsibility, not a collective or governmental necessity.

Our approach march to the line is uneventful. It is ordained that we go for instruction, for a short period, with the 4th Division. We are in luck. I take the left half battalion into the trenches, at Hamel, for six days, during which period we are attached to the 1st battalion the Rifle Brigade, a unit which had consistently added fresh laurels to

an illustrious regimental record ever since it came
into the picture on 25th August, 1914, with the
3rd Army Corps. We are as much a source of interest
to the R.B.'s as they are to us. But to me the one
question is, 'how will the men shape?' Luckily the
line is very quiet, but a stray shell or two, machine-
gun fire at night and all the rest of it, with a casualty
here and there, cannot but do good, for young soldiers
are like young dogs, they require careful shooting
over before being put into the big business. Several
Divisions were unavoidably ruined, almost beyond
repair, by having to attempt to achieve the impossible without the necessary experience.

I see our first man hit. He is a boy of nineteen
years of age. A bit of stray high-explosive shell gets
him in the leg. It was almost an accident, for had
he left me five seconds earlier he would have missed
it. White, calm, uncomplaining, he calls for a
cigarette and is carried off on a stretcher by four
stalwart veterans of the Rifle Brigade. He is never
to return, for amputation follows. Such is war.
Constant training for a whole year and then just one
day in the line! This is attrition! Our time comes
to go back to billets. The Commanding Officer of
the Rifle Brigade speaks well of us; that valiant soul,
Brigadier-General Prouse, pats me on the back as
I pass out. 'Good stuff,' he says nodding to some
men of mine. That is enough. When Prouse says

it's good stuff, it is more than good, it is reliable.
Six hundred of this 'good stuff' are to go West or to
Blighty, in the immortal company of Prouse, within
a few hundred yards of where we stand, nine months
hence, on 1st July, 1916.

We concentrate as a Division behind the lines.
Misfortune overtakes us, which, although seemingly
disastrous, is in reality a blessing in disguise. We
are moving back to the lines. The battalion is formed
up in the roadway in a little village. It is my duty
to report all present, or otherwise, to the Colonel.
Four men are absent! Who are they? I ask the
adjutant. 'All senior sergeants or warrant-officers,'
he replies, giving me the names. 'They are all
lying in an *estaminet* dead drunk on French fire-
water, otherwise doped brandy which it is unlawful
now to sell!' he adds. I report the battalion present,
it is a pity to spoil the Colonel's ride. The quartermaster, Newton, always able to rise to the occasion,
puts the doped men into an ambulance and drives
ahead with them to our destination. They appear at
orderly room next day, to the Colonel's consternation.
Trial by Field General Court Martial, reduction to
the ranks and a long term of imprisonment is the
price of ignorance tempered with folly. These men
had no knowledge of the narcotic power of bad
brandy. They consumed it as if they were drinking
Guinness in their native land! It so happened that

other unfortunate 'accidents,' such as minor looting, take place in other battalions of the brigade at about the same time, with the result that Major-General Oliver Nugent, the newly appointed Divisional Commander, begins to think one of his brigades is an undisciplined mob! As a matter of fact two of the battalions were always much better than the other two, although the men in all the battalions were magnificent. There had been an absence of intellectual and uniform training at the outset, which was often the case in the new armies. General Nugent, taking the bull by the horns, assembles all the officers of our brigade in a village schoolroom where he delivers a strafe, not wholly deserved but very good for us, which I shall always treasure in my mind as the complete example of what can be said by the powerful to the powerless in the shortest space of time possible, consistent with the regulations of words and space for breathing, in the most offensive, sarcastic and uncompromising manner possible. During the harangue I fix my eyes, not to a star but to two stars and a crown, as our senior Colonel Bernard, of the Indian Army, is a full colonel, senior in substantive rank to General Nugent himself! The Colonel's face is a study in parchment, for the Indian sun had tanned and crinkled his skin as is only possible after thirty-three years in the tropics. At last the sentence is pronounced! 'Banishment – to the 4th Division!' We all walk down the street together, my colonel and Bernard leading the way; and have tea with the Indian warrior who remains silent, till all of a sudden, he jumps up and, looking at us, cries: 'Good Lord, we are really in luck. This means we go into the line to *fight* this winter instead of sweeping our way through France in billets!' It is so. We change places with the 12th Brigade of 4th Division and soon take over a sector of our own near Auchonvillers, thus securing priority of service in the line, entry to the leave roster, and invaluable experience, all of which puts us, as a brigade, streets ahead of the other two brigades of the Ulster Division for ever. So well do we get on in the admirable division, commanded by Major-General the Hon. Sir William Lambton, who at the time possesses probably the best staff in France, that when the time comes to return to the fold, reformed perhaps, but by no means penitent, the men respectfully petition to be allowed to remain! That cannot be, however, as Ulster must have its Division!

But I go too fast. We acquire what is probably the best brigade staff in the army. General Withycombe of the 'Koylis;' his old adjutant, Maurice Day, and Teddy Duffin, a Belfast business man, look after our wants and guide our ways.

Arriving at Hedeauville, we are sent next night to

dig in the front line system near Hamel. A couple of companies are required for work under the Royal Engineers. They go off before dusk and later I ride up to see how things are going and to talk to the men. There has been some shelling. In the moonlight I see an officer sitting down. In one hand is a photograph and in the other a flask. 'This is my darling wife,' I hear him say to himself, holding up the picture high for adoration, 'who has shielded me for years.' 'He is drunk,' I think, as I approach. Suddenly all is smoke, dust, stink and dirt. A h.e. shell of heavy calibre has arrived. The air vibrates, the roar is deafening. Then all is calm. 'Any one hurt?' I ask – 'Can't find the officer, Sir,' calls out the sergeant. 'Dig for him like blazes down there,' I order, pointing to a heap of wreckage. They dig like mad and find a bit of cap ('twas before the days of tin helmets), a leg, an arm, a scrap of cardboard, torn, and on it a portion of a photograph. 'I send you the enclosed photograph,' I write home later, to the officer's wife, 'he always thought so much of you and spoke so feelingly of you. This photo was on him when he died.' The shelling continues but the work goes on. I stay with them, it is their first nasty jar. Two days later the Commanding Officer published the following in orders:

'The following has been received from H.Q. 4th Division.

'The Divisional-Commander wishes to express his appreciation of the soldierly bearing under heavy shell fire of the working party of 9th Battalion Royal Irish Rifles. The R.E. officer i/c. work speaks highly of the manner in which the task was completed despite the heavy fire.'

'The first chit,' I laughingly say to Merryman, the sergeant who was on duty. 'Well done!' 'Yes – Sur,' he replies, 'it may be the *furst* but it won't be the last!' He was right.

We move north and occupy a piece of the line taken over recently from the French. It is decided that we work in pairs and that 10th Rifles and ourselves relieve each other. It is as well: had it been otherwise there might have been blood in the wrong trenches! The Colonel and Colonel Bernard toss for who shall go in first. The Indian warrior wins. 'We take first knock, Ormerod,' he says, 'no two bites at a cherry for me!'

Meanwhile, as the tossing is in progress, the medical officer comes into the mess. 'Can I speak to you for a minute, Major?' he asks. 'Yes, O'Brien, what is it?' I reply, walking out with him to the apple orchard. 'I want your help,' he says, 'young Rochdale has venereal, gonorrhoea, in. fact, he's in an awful stew. He's engaged to be married. If I send him down to the venereal hospital it is sure to get out at home where he is.' He pauses. 'Go on,' I say. 'He can be got fairly right in ten days. If he goes to Amiens to one of these French doctors for three or four days and gets a cure – at a price – he may be all right; he could then come back with the dope and treat himself.' 'I don't like the idea of him knocking about here like that,' I say; 'anyhow, I will see what can be done, leave it to me.' After dinner the Colonel and I chat about things and I see my chance. 'Rochdale has very important business to attend to, Colonel,' I say; 'he should really go home, but he doesn't want to. He can get it fixed up in Amiens. We don't go in for ten days: do you mind if I let him go at the first opportunity and give him a pass?' 'Certainly, Crozier, certainly,' assented the C.O. Rochdale returned in ten days' time and took his place in his platoon – cured.

We go in to the trenches for four days, while the weather becomes atrocious. It is notorious that French trenches are seldom good and these are no exceptions. Because there is no revetting, walls of fire and communication trenches fall in, so-called dugouts collapse, and telephone wires connecting companies and brigade become non-effective, consequent on the landslide. The men are up to their waists in mud and water. Rats drown and rations cannot be got up. The Colonel gets a bad cold. We get out, by hook or crook to Mailly-Mailly, the relief taking twelve hours to complete. I had sent my orderly Hackett on ahead to open my kit and get a bed ready. We arrive at 5 a.m., in billets, the Colonel being obviously ill. He is over sixty. A bed has been prepared by the doctor and everything else is fairly comfortable for the old chap. 'Where is Hackett? Where is my bed and billet?' I ask! Starrett, my servant, arrives from the line, after me. 'Hackett is dead drunk,' he says, 'and your kit is still in the store!'

Hackett went back to duty with his company next morning. Four days later he went to sleep, while on listening patrol in no man's land; and some enterprising Germans came along and clubbed him and two others over the head and took the lot of them to Germany, where they spent the rest of the war – wiser and no doubt more sober men!

The day comes for us to return to the line. The doctor and I try to persuade the colonel, who has been in bed all the time since our arrival in billets, to remain out this tour. 'It's your only chance, Sir,' says the good medico, 'you should really be in hospital now.' 'My duty, as you both know, is with my battalion or away from it,' came the reply. 'I am not going away from it, so I must go with it!' And he did! How Colonel Ormerod reached the headquarter dugout in the trenches I do not know. He rode a mile and walked eight hundred yards over the top, in mud, up to his knees, as communication trenches there were none. But it was one thing getting there, another getting out. He lies down at once and remains there for four days. Meanwhile a beam across the dugout roof falls in and knocks him on the back – yet he still holds on. There is not now a proper trench or dugout in the sector, save on the extreme left where the men are in luck and tunnels in a chalky hill and the chalky walls of trenches have stood up.

On our right the machine-gun officer gives trouble. He is not getting the necessary number of rounds off per night. I speak to him. He fears to fire. 'The Boche will see the flash of my guns!' he pleads. 'You must screen them,' I say. A highly-strung timid man, seven months later he went over the top with his guns, and, screwing up his courage, fell fighting hand to hand in the German counter-onslaught, as his brother had done before him at Gallipoli. What men these are! What obstacles they overcome!

I leave Ormerod asleep to go my rounds. There is much to be done the first night in. The doctor keeps an eye on the colonel. Shaking his head seriously, 'I wish to God,' he says,' I had made him go to hospital, it may now be too late.'

The question of the evacuation of the wounded and sick on stretchers becomes more serious, as the mud has made it impossible to clear the cases away. 'Attrition' brings numerous cases of sickness and wounds. The dead don't count, the bodies can wait without enduring pain. Death has its mercies, but to the living, sick and shattered, to them the mud means misery and acute suffering.

It is always quite impossible to get quickly to the left company, commanded by George Gaffikin, by way of the trenches, as there are none, so, followed by Mullins, an ex-sailor, who has become my new orderly, and with electric torch in hand I make for the chalky line, over the top. The going is hard as the mud is deep. Shell holes and huge craters, some ten feet deep, abound and are full of water. To stumble and fall into one of these means death by drowning and suffocation. I light the torch and chance it. Suddenly as I near the front line I hear an angry voice. 'Put that —— light out, you —— ——' 'Sorry,' I reply, 'but you know where you are, and I'm damned if I know where I am, and I'd rather be shot than drowned any night.' 'Beg pardon, Sir,' comes the reply, 'didn't know it was you.' 'That's all right,' I answer cheerfully, 'no harm done.' I jump into the trench and grope my way along. As if by magic a veritable babel greets my ears – Belfast voices, loud, excited and overpowering, fill the air. 'What the devil's all this noise,' I say, 'do you want to be shelled to hell? What are you doing?'

'We're going over the top, Sir,' says a grimy Rifleman.
'Who says so?' says I. 'The captain,' says he. 'Does
he,' says I, 'Why?' 'Two of our fellars is taken
prisoners,' says he, 'an' we've to go and pull them
back!' 'Where's your officer?' I ask. 'Here, Sir,'
comes a voice from the distance. 'What's all this,
Gold?' I ask. 'We have lost two men on patrol,
Sir,' says Gold, 'Capt. Gaffikin ordered two platoons
to go over to fetch them back!' 'Good heavens,'
I reply, 'what's the matter with him, has he gone
mad? Tell these men to get on with their work.
Where is Gaffikin?' 'In his dugout, Sir,' comes the
quick answer. 'Come with me to him,' I mutter.
Now Gold is a very good fellow, no fool, and of
mature years. He follows silently. I enter the chalk
cave which serves as a company headquarters.
Gaffikin's old servant is there. He has done his best.
I see no Gaffikin but I know where the bed is. A
waterproof sheet now hides it. I lift it up. There is
George, asleep. I poke him with my stick. He
moves and grunts. I smell his breath. 'Drunk,'
I say, looking at an almost empty whisky bottle.
I look at Gold. 'Don't let him leave here until
I come back just before stand-to,' I order. 'Take all
the liquor away: also the ammunition.' Gold follows
me out. 'I must go back over the top direct from
here,' I tell him. 'Can you give me a man, I have
sent my fellow back?' I ask. 'Sir,' he says, looking

69

at me straight, 'will you please overlook this? He has had an awful time.' I don't answer. 'He has had an awful time' echoes in my ears as I plod my way with lighted torch towards my headquarters. Suddenly, behind me I hear a thud followed by a splash. I turn round and flash the light. I can see nothing. I search the craters, not a sign, but I see the marks of slipping feet on the lip of a huge shellhole. Gold's man has gone. What can I do? Here I am alone, by measure four hundred yards, perhaps, from either Gold or my own headquarters, by time perhaps one hour, as the mud is deep. 'Anyway what good can anybody do?' I ask myself. Fully equipped and heavily clad, clogged with slime, and held as if in a vice by mud, what chance has any man in such circumstances? Shall I ever know the crater again? What can I leave to mark it? Stones are scarce in muddy valleys. I think of my white handkerchief and lay it out flat on the ground. I scrape up mud with my hands and fasten down the sign. I can do no more. In any case I must go back to headquarters before going to see Gaffikin at stand-to, as the situation report has to be telephoned in at 4 a.m. and I must see how the Colonel is. I wander on alone and hit the main communication trench a hundred yards west of the mark. This means more delay. At length I arrive at our dugout door. The mud and water make a squelching noise as I lift each leg in turn. 'Hush!' says the doctor, placing his finger on his lips; 'the old man's asleep, it's his chance.' I go to the tin-topped cookhouse instead of the dugout so as not to wake him and sit down on an empty case. 'Have this hot tea, Sir,' says Maguirty, the *chef*. 'My God, Maguirty,' I reply, 'you're one in a million, hot tea always ready, you'll receive your reward in heaven!' 'Indeed an' I won't, Sur,' says the good man laughingly. 'It's on earth I'll resave it, God be praised, having the officers well; but, ah, Sur, the poor Colonel, how is he? He's a gran' marn!' At this juncture, Hine, the smart new adjutant, from the East Lancs., who has been in the war since the start, at first as a sergeant in the Grenadiers, interrupts me to say that the brigadier wishes to see me at the junction of Acorn and Apple trenches at 10.30 a.m. 'What do the casualty returns from companies say?' I ask. 'Only two missing, you know of them, and one wounded,' he casually remarks. 'Then put down one drowned of 'B' company. I don't know his name, find it out from Gold: he lent him to me as an orderly.' 'Righto, Sir,' cheerfully says Pokey Die – where he got that nickname or who gave it to him no one knows – but Hine was never known to be anything but cheerful no matter what the circumstances.

After a brief rest I make my way back to Gaffikin across the muddy shell-pocked and water-logged ground. I enter the dugout. George is sitting on his bed, his face covered by his hands, his elbows on his knees. As I approach, the old servant disappears. The officer commanding 'B' company stands up. 'Sit down,' I say and I do likewise, on an old backless kitchen chair, taken from some house. I look at the watch on my wrist – I wear it still – and stare George full in the face, for what seems like five minutes. His eyelids droop, his head bends down. At last I speak. 'Look at me,' I order, and he does so. 'Will you give me your word of honour not to touch liquor again so long as you are with the battalion? I don't care what you do when you're on leave,' I say slowly. 'I will, Sir,' comes the instant reply. 'Right,' I remark, holding out my hand. We go to 'stand-to' together. On the way I pass Gold, anxious, perturbed, and obviously inquisitive. 'Morning, Gold,' I say. He salutes, 'I want you,' I say, 'to tell the men at stand-to that Capt. Gaffikin has been much overcome by the stress of weather and the loss of those two men last night, and that he's coming down to my headquarters to rest for a few hours.' 'Come on George,' I add. Of course, I suppose I should have 'run' Gaffikin; but I knew him and his men. I knew it wouldn't occur again, if he said so. I knew others didn't know much, as he got drunk in his dugout, after the two men were lost, and never left it. Of course, a court martial could only mean one thing – dismissal; and I felt that, although I knew George would enlist as a Tommy if dismissed, he would probably go to the dogs as well, sooner or later. So I took the risk on the less rigid outlook.

It took us three hours to get 'home' by the trenches – or muddy ditches, as they were – for it was now daylight and 'the top' could not be used. 'Look here, George,' I say as we plod along, 'there is one thing certain – while we have been fighting for our lives against mud and water, trench-feet and pneumonia, the Boche have gained the supremacy in 'no man's land.' 'First we lose Hackett and two others; now two more; it must stop.'

George and I have our breakfast together in the one and only dugout, now almost collapsed. Maguirty makes the eggs and bacon taste wonderful, while the jam and tea go down like one o'clock. George is a bit off his feed I notice, probably because eggs and bacon, as well as jam and tea do not mix with unlimited whisky at 10 a.m. as a rule; but I make up for him!

The colonel seems a little better, and he has slept well. George and I gas and talk about home and leave, revues, Paris and everything save war, and I push him off at dusk across the top to his company. Later I go to the handkerchief-marked crater, and by shaded torchlight read a few sentences from the

Burial Service over the muddy grave of my unfortunate guide, to which Mullins says 'Amen.' Soon I pass Harkness on a stretcher in a fire trench. He moans and groans in fearful agony. 'What is it?' I ask. 'A stomach wound,' replies a bearer. I give him a pull at my flask. 'Poor devil,' I muse, 'they now say the brandy will kill him. I did it for the best.'

The fourth day arrives. We are due for relief. A large working party has been put on to the main communication trench by brigade, so now the colonel can be evacuated on a stretcher. The doctor tells him so. 'Me on a stretcher and the battalion walking out! If I am wounded it's different – I walk back to my horse and ride the rest!' says this remarkable man. *And he did!* But it is the last great effort. Arriving in his billet at 2 a.m. next morning, he collapses. An ambulance whisks him to hospital just in time, for pneumonia has set in. Exit Ormerod from the line, but not from the war! Never was a whiter man.

It takes us two days to dry ourselves, sleep, clean and replenish. On the third day I inspect, and on the fourth we go in again. The trenches are a little better, as the rain has ceased. The fog hangs heavy all morning on the first day in. Horace Haslett gets up on to his parados to examine his 'knife rests,' and wire. Meanwhile an enterprising German, having walked across no man's land in the fog, lies down at our front wire, sees Horace a few yards away, and drawing a bead, hits him through the head, gouging out an eye. Truly we must obtain control of the narrow spaces! Old Ormerod all this time is lying on his back in hospital, thinking, thinking, thinking of us; and as he meditates a stretcher is brought in, and on it is an officer. 'A wound casualty?' asks the colonel of his nurse. 'Yes, a young captain in the Royal Irish Rifles, hit through the head; he has lost an eye; he may live, but his condition is very grave,' replies the nurse. Of course the name has to be found out. Haslett is the colonel's pet company commander. Men of faith rarely die in war – if there is the slightest chance of recovery. Haslett wanted to get back to fight, so did Ormerod. I lunched with both in town less than three months after their admission to that casualty clearing station, while on leave. Haslett got back with one eye ten months later.

We start at night to push the Germans out of their snug hiding places in no man's land. 'Daisy' Sinclair bombs a sap. Stevenson and Gold take out strong patrols. We speedily gain command of no man's land. Our luck is in because we side-step to the left. This puts us all on higher ground among the chalk. Our battalion headquarters are luxuriously dry. We have solid earth, as nature made it, on top, capable of keeping out anything, for we are dug into the hill-side. Only fifty yards separates us from the Germans in one place. We mine and they mine – we blow and they blow. What a game it is! Christmas is spent in the line. We give the enemy half an hour's hell with all kinds of guns and weapons as a Christmas box. I do not believe in Christmas relaxation, in war.

On the left the mud is awful up to the Serre road. In the middle is the redan, a tiny salient. The Brigadier decides to give this death trap up and wire the vacated trenches. I go out at night with Ronaldson to reconnoitre. We miss our way. Where are we? Lost? It looks like it. It is a race against time, as, if we are not in our own line by dawn, we must hide all day or get shot. We are in a gigantic crater. We must not slip to the bottom. I pause and think, and try to locate our wire. We strike out once more. A flash, a shot, a bullet whistles round our ears. 'Stop shooting,' I cry. 'Who's that?' comes the answer. 'William of Orange,' I venture, giving the countersign in the hope of recognition. 'Come on then, and let's look at ye,' shouts a savage sentry at the point of the bayonet. 'Oh, it's the colonel,' I hear him say as I crawl forward, for I had been appointed acting lieutenant-colonel that very day – 'William of Orange never lost his way!'

The fight against the condition known as 'trench-feet' had been incessant and an uphill game. However, science and discipline had conquered, and now we seldom have a case, and if we do there is trouble. Socks are changed and dried in the line, thigh boots are worn and are dried every four days when we come out. Things are better, but the weather gets worse.

Evidently men in other places have taken to blowing off their fingers to escape service in the line, as all self-inflicted 'accidental' wounds of any sort are to be made the subject of legal proceedings against the wounded. Our sergeant-major, an excellent soldier, throws a bit of brass into a brazier. It is a detonator! It explodes and inflicts damage on his hand! He goes to hospital, is tried by court martial and reduced to the rank of sergeant. Returning at once, I make him *acting* sergeant-major, which is not the same, though the best I can do, as, although he receives the pay of a sergeant-major, he will lose his rank and pay if wounded. His family will suffer. War is stern. The innocent as well as the guilty must suffer.

One morning I go down to the right to meet Colonel Bernard at our junction, in order to decide a tactical consideration. We are to meet at 10 a.m. I wait. The colonel is late, a most unusual thing for him. I stay on till 11 a.m. and am on the point of departure when I hear a sound. I look up. What do

I see? It is Bernard all right, but he walks gingerly. What has he got on? Socks, shirt, tunic, cap, nothing else! He roars with laughter as he approaches. I regard him with amazement! 'You may well look,' he says, 'I got bogged. Luckily they heard me. My trench boots were wedged, so they pulled me out of them. I had slacks on in order to free the circulation, so I undid the braces and thigh straps and got them to pull me out of the lot. Your H.Q. is nearer than mine, so I have told them to send me along a pair of breeks and some boots!' As it is very cold we move on to dry ground in a hollow and make for my dugout, my orderly carrying the colonel on his back, as his feet are cut.

That evening Paddy Jackson comes up from the base with a draft. He was too young to come out with us. He dines (!) with me and goes up to see his old company. Anxious to see all the fun, he goes out on patrol and takes part in a scrap, later returning to the base. Seven months later he is wounded when with us, but, returning, faces the music once more, this time to die! It is to boys like this that England owes her greatness.

To the isolated left I plod next morning. Posts are few and far between. Rounding a traverse I hear a rifle crack quite near. A few paces on and I find a corpse, quite warm. A hole in the head and not much blood. Beside is a muddy rifle in the slush.

I open the breech and extract an empty cartridge case. The cut-off is closed. I tumble to it! Fed up with the mud and general beastliness, afraid to flee lest he should be caught, as he surely would be, and shot by his comrades in accordance with the rules of war, unable to endure the conditions any longer, he ends his days by his own hand. I say nothing, save to give some unknown German sniper credit for a good shot he never fired, for we have long since silenced the marksmen across the way.

That afternoon I go to the right and am told Felucan, an elderly subaltern, has been evacuated as a casualty. Wrongly based on whisky in civilian life, he has resorted to it again in order to keep going. He is not drunk. He can never get drunk! A bottle is found in his valise. His nerves are awful. He is quite unsafe and a bad example. We are well rid of him though I am sorry for him, as I like him. I push along and come to a sentry. Beside him a boot sticks out of the parapet and on it hangs a water bottle. 'Why do you hang that there,' I ask, 'do you know what it is?' 'Yes Sir,' the youth replies, 'a dead Frenchman.' 'Well,' I say, 'if you put weight on it the whole thing will come down and then you'll have an awful business.' He takes the water bottle off its human hook and places it else-where. We are on an old French battlefield – hence the big rats and half buried *poilus* which abound

79

throughout our area. Later, when the warmth arrives, the stench from decomposed bodies becomes so great that we have to sprinkle disinfectants on the ground. One officer is evacuated suffering from blood poisoning, a rat having bitten him on the nose, while asleep. We are worse than scavengers! War is a dirtier game than is generally known. I go on leave for ten days and enjoy every moment of the time, save the parting; and as the coming back is always so bad, I sometimes hesitate to go on leave at all as each parting grows worse, instead of better.

The old redan has become a veritable hell-hole, as it is easily reached by hostile mortar fire. In February, George Gaffikin holds it and we are attacked. We are ready. The artillery receive our secret Very light signal and hell is let loose. George keeps his head and as a reward is personally mentioned in Sir Douglas Haig's first despatch in June, as is also the whole battalion. Later, an officer, Rochdale by name, who once went to Amiens for ten days on private business, is sitting in the redan dugout at 2 a.m. with his company commander. I enter. They show me a peculiar German rifle grenade and say it is of new design. As Rochdale understands bombs I suggest he takes it down and examines it when we come out to rest. He agrees. The big trench mortars then start. Everything is

shaken, including Rochdale's nerves. We are short
of subalterns. Rochdale has been sent out earlier
to put a notice on the German wire, by order of
Corps headquarters, a propagandic move to inform
the front line men that their families are starving
at home. Now the trench mortaring is too much for
him. He rises, rushes past me, and bolts down the
trench in front of his men as fast as he can go. After
daylight he is discovered in a disused French dugout
behind the lines, asleep – apparently a deserter, as
absence and evasion of duty are the two chief
factors which go to constitute the offence. There is
the additional fact that he has shown apparent
cowardice in action, in front of his men. It is just as
futile to be half a mile away from the duty point as
sixty kilometres. I have already a private soldier
absent. He will no doubt be caught and tried.
What about this officer? I see him and put him
back for trial by court martial for cowardice and
desertion. He is tried and found guilty of one charge
or both. Meanwhile the private – Crocker – is caught
by the military police, a long way back. He too is
tried. I sign the charge sheet of both these men.
Promulgation, where death sentences occur, is a long
and painful job. One day we received a wire.
Rochdale is to be 'released from arrest and all consequences.' They try to send him back to duty but
I refuse to receive him. I am asked my opinion as

to whether sentence of death should be carried out
on Crocker. In view of certain circumstances I
recommend the shooting be carried out. At last
I receive the orders and documents relative to the
execution. We leave the line for four days' rest at
Mailly-Mailly.

In the afternoon of the first day out we parade in
hollow square. The prisoner – Crocker – is produced. Cap off he is marched by the sergeant-major
to the centre. The adjutant reads the name, number,
charge, finding, sentence and confirmation by Sir
Douglas Haig. Crocker stands erect. He does not
flinch. Perhaps he is dazed: who would not be?
The prisoner is marched away by the regimental
police while I, placing myself at the head of the
battalion, behind the band, march back to billets.
The drums strike up, the men catch step. We all
feel bad but we carry out our war-time pose. Crocker
didn't flinch, why should we? After tea the padre
comes to see me. 'Might I see Crocker?' he asks.
'Of course, Padre, but don't be too long-winded,'
I say seriously, 'after you have done anything you
can for him tell his company commander. But
I don't think his people should be told. He can go
into the 'died' return. War is all pot-luck, some get
a hero's halo, others a coward's cross. But this man
volunteered in '14. His heart was in the right place
then, even if his feet are cold in '16. What do you

say?' 'I quite agree,' answers the good man, much too overcome to say more.

Now, in peace time, I and the rest of us would have been very upset indeed at having to shoot a colleague, comrade, call him what you will, at dawn on the morrow. We would not, in ordinary circumstances, have slept. Now the men don't like it but they have to put up with it. They face their ordeal magnificently. I supervise the preliminary arrangements myself. We put the prisoner in a comfortable warm place. A few yards away we drive in a post, in a back garden, such as exists with any villa residence. I send for a certain junior officer and show him all. 'You will be in charge of the firing party,' I say, 'the men will be cold, nervous and excited, they may miss their mark. You are to have your revolver ready, loaded and cocked; if the medical officer tells you life is not extinct you are to walk up to the victim, place the muzzle of the revolver to his heart and press the trigger. Do you understand?' 'Yes Sir,' came the quick reply. 'Right,' I add, 'dine with me at my mess to-night.' I want to keep this young fellow engaged under my own supervision until late at night, so as to minimise the chance of his flying to the bottle for support. As for Crocker, he leaves this earth, in so far as knowing anything of his surroundings is concerned, by midnight, for I arrange that enough spirituous liquor is left beside him to sink a ship. In the morning, at dawn, the snow being on the ground, the battalion forms up on the public road. Inside the little garden on the other side of the wall, not ten yards distant from the centre of the line, the victim is carried to the stake. He is far too drunk to walk. He is out of view save from myself, as I stand on a mound near the wall. As he is produced I see he is practically lifeless and quite unconscious. He has already been bound with ropes. There are hooks on the post; we always do things thoroughly in the Rifles. He is hooked on like dead meat in a butcher's shop. His eyes are bandaged – not that it really matters, for he is already blind. The men of the firing party pick up their rifles, one of which is unloaded, on a given sign. On another sign they come to the *Present* and, on the lowering of a handkerchief by the officer, they fire – a volley rings out – a nervous ragged volley it is true, yet a volley. Before the fatal shots are fired I had called the battalion to attention. There is a pause, I wait. I see the medical officer examining the victim. He makes a sign, the subaltern strides forward, a single shot rings out. Life is now extinct. We march back to breakfast while the men of a certain company pay the last tribute at the graveside of an unfortunate comrade. This is war.

To this sad story there was a sequel. Some months

later one of my officers was on leave, and as he had recently been awarded the D.S.O. was entertained to luncheon by his Club. At the function there were present some young business men who had not volunteered for war service. One of these asked my officer if it were true that 'one of your men had been executed for desertion, and if so did he not think it was a very discreditable affair for the battalion and a disgrace to the city?' 'Well,' my officer replied, 'the unfortunate man volunteered to serve his country in the field; you have .not done even that yet. He went through the trials of a truly terrible winter in the trenches. He endured bombardment, mud, exposure, cold, frost, trench-feet, sleepless nights and daily drudgery under conditions in which man was never intended to play a part (he had to play a part the whole time to keep going at all). This quite unnatural test broke his spirit. His brain was probably affected. In despair he quitted the line. Why don't you and your other slacking and pro-fiteering friends join up and have a shot at doing better than this unhappy comrade of ours? If you can't stand the test and are executed because you are not endowed with the steel-like qualities which make for war efficiency, I shall think better of you than I do now. Our dead comrade, whom we had to kill with our own hands and rifles *pour encourager les autres*, is a hero compared with you! He tried and failed. He died for such as you! Isn't it time you had a shot at dying for your country?'

On St. Patrick's Day we receive shamrock from Mr. John Redmond, and in replying express a hope that he will wear Orange lilies from us on the 12th of July, for luck! We also send a telegram to our old colonel, 'Your flag is still flying high.' It was never lowered. In the meantime that wonderful old soldier has made a marvellous recovery, and has actually been passed fit again for service in France! The divisional commander, thinking it unwise that the doughty veteran should return, causes him to be stopped on the boat at Southampton. Colonel Ormerod commanded a reserve battalion and a prisoner-of-war camp until 1919, a grateful country awarding him nothing for his unique service – while skrimshankers waxed fat.

The glorious spring is now on us. The 4th Division have gone to rest while the Ulster Division has taken over the area. Rumour has it that we are to be relieved, and well we might be. During the winter our little area has been the scene of tragedy, comedy, heroics, valour, fortitude, and endurance which few men could have accomplished, save for the effective victory of mind over matter, as expressed in the two words 'intellectual discipline,' and for the saving grace of humour. There had been no battle, yet we lost heavily. What is there to show? A clean slate! Enhanced experience! A knowldege that the acid test is soon to be applied and that when it comes we shall not be found wanting! We are relieved by a division from the East. They know nothing of this country or of the enemy or of the requirements of either! Some come in for instruction in advance. We leave officers and N.C.O.'s behind to help. By day these new soldiers wash, shave, strip, take off their equipment and boots, have baths, sing songs, play cards and sleep in the front line. They never work! At nightfall they become uneasy. They are careless by day and 'windy' by night. They evidently do not know the trenches are an outpost line. One nice boy, whom I leave behind to show the ropes, is scandalously killed by one of their sentries. A subaltern at an early age he gave much promise. It is bad enough to be shot by the enemy, that is expected; but one expects to be immune from the bullets of one's own side, under normal war conditions, although I did once hear a warrior say he didn't care a hang who shot him as long as they made a good quick job of it!

# CHAPTER IV

## THE ACID TEST

I HAVE experienced many joys in my life, and I have had my full share of sorrows; but I do not believe any pleasure comes up to that feeling of contentment which arises from the knowledge that one is out for rest in some dingy, insanitary, perhaps unhealthy billet, in some little-heard-of and out-of-the-way village or farm, after a long period of muddy service in the line during winter. We are now nearer to primitive man, as, in a way, we have even deteriorated since 1914. We of the shambles require less for the restoration of our tired frames than do those of the other '*corps d'élite*'– the popinjays and parasites of war, who live and lunch as they have never done before in places previously quite beyond them, thanks to Germany. Such are my feelings as I wake up at a farm near Beauval having left the trenches behind in order to rest, train and renovate my battalion prior to its participation in what was to be one of the greatest battles of our days. I decide to have a battalion mess once more, as I can then

THE BRITISH FRONT LINE AFTER THE GERMAN COUNTER ATTACK AT THIEPVAL, JULY, 1916

regain the grip which is inevitably lost in the system of decentralised messing of the line, and without which war cannot be successfully waged. Jim Newton, the quartermaster, knowing this, gets things going in an instant.

After mess the first night I say a few words as follows: 'I am anxious that training should be in the mornings and that one hour of steady drill should be included so far as is possible. Afternoons will be set aside for organised games. There will be loading parties at railhead and the shell dumps, and there must be no slacking in the performance of this duty. A chit from a loading officer is as commendable as a chit for work in the line. On the shells our future depends. One officer per company can go to the nearest town or any such place, with a pass signed by the adjutant, every day after lunch, returning by midnight. Several officers have asked for leave for Paris; none can be granted except to married officers whose wives may visit Paris for a stipulated number of days. The adjutant knows all about it, as he has only been married three months himself. Concert parties, etc., are being arranged for the men. They must be given as good a time as possible. Remember the venereal question. The medical officer is going to lecture each company tomorrow on that subject and will explain the arrangements he is making for both officers and men.

He will speak to officers separately about their own affairs.'

We spend a very happy two months out of the line, working hard, playing hard, and practising the attack for the battle of the Somme over spit-locked trenches which had been prepared by Tom Foy, who had been attached to the brigade headquarters for a long time for engineering work.

A very good-looking boy, Jimmy Law, a protégé of mine, had become orderly officer to the general. I know his mother and had got him his commission from the ranks in which he had enlisted from school in August, 1914. I used to be anxious about him in the early days, as he was very young, attractive-looking and manly. With the general I felt he was in good hands, as a brigade mess exists at all times and it is in mess that touch is kept. Many a bad old captain ruins his subalterns in the company mess, and in clubs, by his example, conversation, behaviour with women, and drinking habits generally. We know it. It is sad but almost inevitable. In peace time boys do not now often attempt to keep pace with or copy coarse-minded men, and if they do there is often someone to warn them. The senior officers are *in loco parentis* in this emergency and they don't – or won't – see it. I hear coarse remarks in clubs, on the leave boats, in Boulogne hotels and in London, made by middle-aged roués, dressed up in uniform, which would horrify the parents of these young people if they knew. At a certain house in London, officers of all ages were found dancing, retiring, drinking and love-making with girls in government employ, under quite extraordinary circumstances. War brings all these things in its train. All is not gold that glitters.

A boy, fresh from school, became an officer, went to France, and was wounded. After recovery he was posted to a reserve battalion, and there it was that a great deal of the mischief took place. While there, and when he was nineteen years of age, he met a prostitute to whom he was introduced by his captain. They went off together for a week-end. Later, the woman told the lad she was going to become a mother and that he would be the father. He believed her and married her, as he was the soul of honour! She never had a child at all. This boy was the heir to vast estates. His father, a country squire, on being told of the calamity, sent for them both, glanced at the woman, kicked them both out of the house, disinherited the son, and, after the war, sent him a hundred-pound note with which to go to the colonies. There are dozens of cases of this sort for which the war is alone to blame.

To get back to a more pleasant subject, let us follow the battalion into the line, where there are no loose women and but little liquor. The training

for the great attack is complete. It is May. Thiepval
Wood is at its best. The foliage is still unspoilt,
save on the fringe. Birds sing and squirrels jump
from tree to tree.

By this time I could turn on my emotions and
regulate my mental requirements for war, as one
regulates the heat in a railway carriage; 'hot' for
blood-lust action, 'cold' for cool calculation, and
'warm' for recreation and creative power. I have
by now become kaleidoscopic – a mere war freak.
Occasionally, we go back to Martinsart Wood for
rest. The tours in the trenches are now often of
long duration, as the weather is warm. When 'out,'
I have a company, in close support, on Speyside,
above the River Ancre, commanded by a warrior
of twenty-two years of age. He has with him three
subalterns all under nineteen. One day when at
Martinsart, where the nightingales keep me awake
at night, within a few yards of a heavy gun, I ride
up to have tea with these four boys. They have
nothing much to do. The bathing pool is good. As
I arrive they are all standing stark naked on the
improvised spring board, ready to jump in for a race.
How wonderful they look, hard, muscular, fit,
strong and supple, yet devoid of all coarseness.
They ask me to start them and I comply with their
request. As they fix their eyes on me and wait for
the word 'go,' I realise I am, thanks to circumstances,

in the presence not only of boys versed in war, but men already known to women. I think as I watch them ducking each other in the water, and playing like young seals I have so often seen up North, 'what a pity they are not married in order that they might plant their seed.' Mankind has ordained that they shall shortly die. Alas! the weaklings and shirkers escape and breed like rabbits, while the strong suffer and are wiped out.

We are in the line on the 4th of June. There is an old Etonian with us. He is quite a child. He would like to go to the old Etonian dinner at Amiens. I have no objection, providing his company commander doesn't mind; but subalterns are few and he must come back that night. A car arrives across the Ancre to take him to his gathering. Early on the morning of 5th, at 1 a.m., the enemy puts down a big barrage on to the front line. I take cover behind a traverse. In one of those momentary lulls which invariably arise when big business is in progress I hear a drawling voice behind a barricade remark in quiet and serious tones 'I saw no whores in Amiens!' 'Ha, ha,' replies his companion, 'you didn't know where to look, old chap.' Our Etonian has returned; true to his promise he is back in time. *Floreat Etona!* A shell which burst close to them and covered both with earth and fumes, puts an end to this conversation.

All the trenches and strong points in Thiepval Wood are called after Highland places. I am thus enabled, for once, to rule over Gordon Castle, while Elgin Avenue, Speyside, and Blair Atholl remind me of happier days spent killing grouse instead of Germans. We are however lucky, as, although the shelling at night is intense we are well dug in and our casualties, though high, might well be worse. An old school friend, a battalion commander of another force, comes to see me. I take him up Elgin Avenue. He is not long from home, and is obviously ill at ease and timid, and does not understand the ropes. In the avenue, which is a main communication trench, we pass a rifleman carrying a sandbag full of something. I become suspicious. Thefts of rations and minor stores and comforts from the line are increasing. 'What have you got in that bag?' I ask. 'Rifleman Gundy,' comes the unexpected answer. He is carrying down the only mortal remains of Gundy for decent burial in a bag which measures a few feet by inches! My friend looks puzzled and I explain. I see he is obviously upset and nervous. He is not used to big battle, let alone normal inactivity. We wander on and our luck remains out, for, at the junction of Elgin Avenue and the fire trench we meet a man with a human arm in his hand. 'Whose is that?' I ask. 'Rifleman Broderick's, Sir,' is the reply. 'Where's

Broderick?' is my next question. 'Up there, Sir,' says my informant, pointing to a tree top above our heads. There sure enough is the torn trunk of a man fixed securely in the branches of a shell-stripped oak. A high explosive shell has recently shot him up to the sky and landed him in mid air above and out of reach of his comrades. This is too much for my companion, who desires to go back. 'Well,' I tell him, 'anyhow we won't stand here at the junction of these trenches; junctions and cross roads are always bad places. Come along down here. We will go down to Montey's dugout, and get back another way.' He is reluctant, for he doesn't know what I know. It is time for Elgin to be shelled; the Boche, with all his knowledge, is surprisingly regular in some of his habits. No, he will go back the way he came! 'If you do, you may cop it!' I say. He follows me. We reach the dugout and I introduce my friend. Montey, with his usual hospitality, offers a drink, which is gladly accepted. 'I have tea for you, Sir,' he knowingly remarks. Just as we are in the middle of exchanging sweet pleasantries shells begin to burst up and down Elgin Avenue, a hundred yards away. My friend jumps in his seat. 'Where is that?' he asks. 'In Elgin Avenue where you wanted to go,' I reply. He pauses and says nothing. The firing stops. We get up to leave. I make for Elgin Avenue. 'Look here,' says my friend, 'you said you'd go the other way, why don't you?' 'Because,' I laughingly reply, 'Elgin is safer now, the other way is worse, it may get it soon!' 'How the devil do you know all these things?' he pleadingly asks. 'Don't you know I am supposed to know everything that goes on in this wood?' I reply. 'I give it up,' he says, shaking his head, 'this is no place for a white man.' 'Of course it isn't,' I emphatically proclaim; 'all the world knows that, but mankind put us here, and there's only one way out, through that part of mankind over there,' pointing to the enemy!

Mid June, 1916, sees us back near Forceville, polishing up the book of words of the 'Acid Test.' I lecture the whole battalion in a big barn, aided by a cloth map twenty feet square which has been prepared by Major Woods, now second-in-command, a draughtsman by profession. I hear each company commander lecture his company in the same way. We are word-perfect. Will our acting be as good? Shall we play our parts as well? It is a big drama which is about to be produced. In our own part of the stage alone, there are eight hundred players! There is no chorus. There are no supers. Each one of us has an important individual part to play. Unfortunately, the audience is liable to object and thus upset the players! That is how I put the problem to over eight hundred men of good faith.

It is no task of mine to describe the tactical considerations of the great battle of the Somme which
opened on 1st July, 1916, or to follow the handling
of the men who took part in it. If the reader wishes,
he can follow the movements of such men as
Bernard, Gaffikin, Woods, and even myself, in
detail, in Sir Arthur Conan Doyle's *British Campaigns of Europe*. For me it is to record our feelings,
sayings and doings on that great day. The battle
story opens in Aveluy Wood, on the evening of
June 30th, where our brigade is assembled. We are
to attack next morning. I spend much of the night
with Colonel Bernard resting against a tree trunk,
eating sandwiches and drinking tea. He is dubious
of the success of the assault on Thiepval village by
the division on our right. 'If that fails,' he says,
'where are we on the flank?' We agree, if we see,
on marching through Thiepval Wood, that Thiepval
village is still in enemy hands, we shall meet in
no man's land, to alter our plans, if necessary.
If only one of us arrives there, then it will be up
to him to carry on for both battalions. If neither
of us gets as far, then the senior officers present will
carry on. This they are told, and then we change the
subject. 'I hope,' says the colonel, 'this war will
settle the Irish question. The Ulster and the Irish
Divisions, shoulder to shoulder in France, should
consolidate the home front afterwards, despite the

Rebellion. I know nothing of politics,' he adds,
'I hate them – they are the curse of every land; but
I know the Irish Question is an unreal politically-
inspired game of bluff and office-seeking expediency.
Good night, old chap,' he says, 'I must get some
sleep.' It is the last 'Good night,' he is to say, for
nine hours later he goes to his long rest to join the
vast legion of happy warriors. I move over to my
saddlebags and lie down to sleep. My mind goes
back to the Tugela where I did much the same thing
sixteen years ago, as a mere lad, before the final
advance to Ladysmith. Sleep does not come. I
wander about among the men, who are all lying on
the ground, their arms piled, their equipment ready.
Most are asleep. I talk to some in lowered tones
who are looking at the stars in contemplation. Reaching the fringe of the wood on the northern side, I
see a light. True, it is dimmed, but there are orders
against showing any lights, lest hovering enemy
aircraft might detect or surmise the presence of the
assembled troops. 'Put that light out,' I order.
'Don't you know you shouldn't have a light?' I add.
'Do you want to give the whole show away?' I
indignantly ask. 'I am writing a letter home, Sir,
it will be my last, and I just feel like it,' says an
apologetic voice, adding, 'I am very sorry, Sir, I
shouldn't have done it.' It's young Campbell, a
stout lad. 'All right,' I say, 'no harm's done,

luckily; but one can't be too careful with other people's lives. If they get wise that we are here they would guess the attack was coming tomorrow, and would be waiting in their trenches with their rifles at the present for our fellows. But why do you say it will be your last letter?' I ask. 'I feel I'm for it, Sir,' he said. 'One day's as good as another, and the sooner the better; all we fellows are bound to get it in the neck, sooner or later. This my first big show. I had a first-rate leave a month ago, and made the best of it, so now I don't mind.' 'Oh, I expect you'll be all right,' I say. 'What about that letter; do you want it posted?' I ask. 'It's a green envelope, Sir, I should like it posted if you could manage it. It is addressed,' he says. 'Give it to me,' I say, holding out my hand, 'I'll get it off first opportunity. Newton is going back at dawn to the stores.' I put the letter in my pocket and move off to my shelter. Dawn breaks. The birds begin to sing. Not another sound is to be heard. The company cooks start to get a move on: they are always the first up. I think I'll get a drop of tea in advance of the rest, so walk over to the cookers. 'Good morning, Sir,' says Day, 'A' company's cook-in-chief. 'Morning, Day. Any tea going?' I ask. 'Surely Sir,' says the good man, picking up a mess tin which he proceeds to clean out with grass. I drink. It's tea all right! Soldiers' tea! Strong, sweet, hot and most welcome.

'What have you got for them for breakfast?' I ask. 'Rashers, fried bread, jam, Sir,' says the worthy man; 'they should be able to fight on that all right; and each man is to have cold tea and lemon in his water bottle,' he adds proudly. 'You're wonderful,' I say, 'and all within twelve hundred yards of the enemy!'

Here and there I see the men get up and stretch. The officers are shaving. Starrett brings me some hot water to do the same. Jimmy Law comes round from Brigade with a chronometer to synchronise the time, as everything has to be done to the second as we are all most punctilious in all that pertains to the destruction of ourselves and others. 'Don't you go and get shot to-day, Jimmy; your mother would never forgive me, and I rashly promised her you would get home in September,' I raggingly say to him. 'The general just told me, Sir, you would kill him if I got in the way of anything harder than my head!' he replies, 'Well, if you do apparently there will be a double murder,' I say, 'so mind out.'

The whistle blows. The men fall in, in fours, in their companies, on the Hamel-Albert Road. The battalion is reported present! Zero hour is at 7.30 a.m. All is quiet on the western front. It is now 6.45 a.m. A pin could be heard to drop. In three-quarters of an hour's time an inferno will

RUINS OF THIEPVAL VILLAGE. AFTER THE BATTLE

have begun which will never cease until the mud of winter and the shortened days call a halt in Picardy and put a temporary stop to carnage. I place myself at the head of the valiant gang. How proud I am. Just before we move off for Speyside under the steep bank of which we are to shelter, Woods, my second-in-command comes up. 'March with me,' I say, 'the nearer the better as I have some things to tell you.' At that moment a colonel approaches. I know him. His face is as white as death. 'Look at his face,' I say to Woods, 'what's wrong with him?' I ask. 'He fears death,' says the dry Ulsterman; 'but not as much as I do!' he adds, with a laugh. I blow my whistle. We're off across the causeways of the Ancre. Thanks to our supremacy in the air, which has cost us countless noble young lives, not a German machine is in sight. Maurice Day, the brigade major, cheery as ever, meets us as we reach the wood, just to strike a lively note. Two German shells drop in the water twenty yards to our left. Is that chance or do they suspect? Ranging perhaps, for future use; but they have no observation from above or on the ground; our Flying Corps has seen to that. A dense mist from the marshes has, in any case, made observation difficult. We turn left. We have gone to Speyside 'tail first,' for 'A' company has to lead out. I let all pass and follow 'A.' Dear old Bernard comes up with his little lot and snuggles in on our right as he has to lead off at 8 a.m. to clear us for our advance.

Suddenly the air is rent with deafening thunder; never has such man-made noise been heard before! The hour has struck! 7.30 a.m. has arrived. The first wave goes over, 'carrying the creeping barrage on its back.' We wait. Instantly the enemy replies, putting down a counter-barrage which misses us by inches. Thanks to the steep slope of Speyside we are immune. That half hour is the worst on record, for thoughts and forebodings; so we sing, but it is difficult to keep in tune or rhythm on account of the noise. At last *our* minute, *our own* minute arrives. I get up from the ground and whistle. The others rise. We move off, with steady pace. As we pass Gordon Castle we pick up coils of wire and iron posts. I feel sure in my innermost thoughts these things will never be carried all the way to the final objective; however, even if they get half way it will be a help. Then I glance to the right through a gap in the trees. I see the 10th Rifles plodding on and then my eyes are riveted on a sight I shall never see again. It is the 32nd division at its best. I see rows upon rows of British soldiers lying dead, dying or wounded, in no man's land. Here and there I see an officer urging on his followers. Occasionally I can see the hands thrown up and then a body flops to the ground. The bursting shells and smoke make visibility poor, but I see enough to convince me Thiepval village is still held, for it is now 8 a.m. and by 7.45 a.m. it should have fallen to allow of our passage forward on its flank. Bernard was right. My upper lip is stiff, my jaws are set. We proceed. Again I look southward from a different angle and perceive heaped up masses of British corpses suspended on the German wire in front of the Thiepval stronghold, while live men rush forward in orderly procession to swell the weight of numbers in the spider's web. Will the last available and previously detailed man soon appear to do his futile duty unto death on the altar of sacrifice? We march on – I lose sight of the 10th Rifles and the human corn-stalks, falling before the Reaper. My pace unconsciously quickens, for I am less heavily burdened than the men behind me, and at last I see the light of day through the telescopic-like avenue which has been cut for our approach. We are nearing the fringe of the wood and the old fire trench. Shells burst at the rate of six a minute on this trench junction, for we have been marching above Elgin Avenue and alongside it. My adjutant, close behind me, tells me I am fifty yards in front of the head of the column. I slacken my pace and they close up to me. 'Now for it,' I say to Hine, 'it's like sitting back for an enormous fence.' My blood is up and I am literally seeing red. Still the shells burst at the head of Elgin, plomp, plomp – it is 'good-bye,' I think, as there is no way round. 'This way to eternity,' shouts a wag behind. Thirty yards ahead now, still a shell – plomp – a splinter flies past my shoulder, and embeds itself in the leg of a leading man behind. He falls and crawls out of the way, nothing must stop the forward march of the column. 'Lucky b——,' says one of his pals, 'you're well out of it, Jimmy, good luck to you, give 'em our love, see you later,' and so the banter continues. It's the only way. The blood swells in my veins. God is merciful, and it almost seems as though he chloroforms us on these occasions. I cross the fire trench. The next shell and I should have absolutely synchronised. It does not arrive! 'What's up?' I think. Still once more too far ahead, I wait on the edge of the wood. They close up once more. I double out to see what's up on the right. Bernard, where is he? Machine guns open fire on us from Thiepval village; their range is wrong: 'too high,' I say to Hine. I survey the situation still; more machine-gun fire: they have lowered their sights: *pit*, *pit*, the bullets hit the dry earth all round. The shelling on to the wood edge has ceased. The men emerge. A miracle has happened. 'Now's the chance,' I think to myself, 'they must quicken pace and get diagonally across to the sunken road, disengaging from each other quickly, company by company.' I stand still and erect in the

open, while each company passes. To each commander I give the amended order. Men are falling
here and there, but the guns previously firing on
the edge of the wood are quite silent. First passes
'A' with Montey at its head. His is the longest
double to the flank. George Gaffikin comes next
waving an orange handkerchief. 'Good-bye, Sir,
good luck,' he shouts to me, *en passant*, 'tell them I
died a teetotaller, put it on the stone if you find me.'
'Good luck, George,' I say, 'don't talk rot, anyhow
you played the game!' He died that day after
behaving with magnificent courage and fortitude
when stricken down. The baby captain of 'C'
comes next. Never demonstrative, he thinks the
more, and passes on to play his part until he finds
himself in a casualty clearing station with Montey,
later. 'D' brings up the rear with Berry at its head.
Imagine a timed exposure with your camera. The
button is pressed, the shutter opens, another press
and it again shuts. That is what happened to us.
The German shelling ceased for five minutes, we
hurried through the gap of mercy, and as Major
Woods, bringing up the rear, was just clear of Elgin,
the shelling started again. Most of the men were
spared for a further few hours of strenuous life that
day. Berry is badly wounded, and, with Gold, later
finds himself in Germany. On the 3rd, I report him
killed. Men have seen him lying dead. They are

positive. Men in battle see fairies – and devils. He is found in Germany through the Geneva organisation, much to my surprise. His people write me an indignant letter asking me what I meant by saying he is dead! The war has made men's minds distorted. I send a postcard back: 'Why not count your blessings?'

The battalion is now formed up lying down on the road. They are enfiladed from Thiepval village while field guns open on them from the front. They can't stay here. Where is Colonel Bernard? I walk over to find out. I find a few men of the 10th, and attach them to the right of my line. I blow shrill whistle calls and signal the advance. They go on their last journey. 'Bunny' (mentioned in Chapter I), now a captain, comes up to me. He has lost his way. I set him on his path. Later he dies at the head of his company. And what of the dead and wounded? This spirited dash across no man's land, carried out as if on parade, has cost us some fifty dead and seventy disabled. The dead no longer count. War has no use for dead men. With luck they will be buried later; the wounded try to crawl back to our lines. Some are hit again in so doing, but the majority lie out all day, sun-baked, parched, uncared for, often delirious and at any rate in great pain. My immediate duty is to look after the situation and not bother about wounded men. I send a message to brigade and move to my battle headquarters in the wood. It is a deep dug-out which has been allocated to me for my use. It needs to be deep to keep out heavy stuff. The telephone lines are all cut by shell fire. Kelly, a burly six-feet-two-inches-high Irish Nationalist, has been sent in a week before to look after emergency rations. He has endured the preliminary bombardment for a week already with the dead and dying, during which time he has had difficulty in going outside, even at night and then only between the shells. A wrong thing has been done. I find the place full of dead and wounded men. It has been used as a refuge. None of the wounded can walk. There are no stretchers. Most are in agony. They have seen no doctor. Some have been there for days. They have simply been pushed down the steep thirty-feet-deep entrance out of further harm's way and left – perhaps forgotten. As I enter the dugout I am greeted with the most awful cries from these dreadfully wounded men. Their removal is a Herculean task, for it was never intended that the dying and the helpless should have to use the deep stairway. After a time, the last sufferer and the last corpse are removed. Meanwhile I mount the parapet to observe. The attack on the right has come to a standstill; the last detailed man has sacrificed himself on the German wire to the God of War. Thiepval village is masked with a wall of corpses.

The adjutant of the 10th tells me Colonel Bernard is no more. The colonel and half his men walked into the barrage of death during the advance. All died behind him as he resolutely faced the edge of the wood in an impossible effort to walk through a wall of raining iron and lead, which had lifted for us that brief five minutes.

All at once there is a shout. Someone seizes a Lewis gun. 'The Germans are on us' goes round like wildfire. I see an advancing crowd of field grey. Fire is opened at six hundred yards range. The men behind the guns have been with Bernard in the shambles. Their nerves are utterly unstrung. The enemy fall like grass before the scythe. 'Damned —— ——' shouts an officer, 'give them hell.' I look through my glasses. 'Good heavens,' I shout, 'those men are prisoners surrendering, and some of our own wounded men are escorting them! Cease fire, cease fire, for God's sake,' I command. The fire ripples on for a time. The target is too good to lose. 'After all they are only Germans,' I hear a youngster say. But I get the upper hand at last – all is now quiet – for a few moments. The tedium of the battle continues.

I hear a rumour about Riflemen retiring on the left and go out to 'stop the rot.' At the corner of Elgin I wait to head them off. Meanwhile I see a German soldier, unarmed, sitting at a newly made shell hole. I ask him if he speaks English. He does. He was once a waiter at Bude in Cornwall. He is fed up with the war, and glad to be where he is. I advise him to move away, or he will not be there long as his countrymen shell that place badly. He thanks me. I offer him a cigarette. His eyes light up. He does not smoke although he takes it. I ask him why. He points to his throat. 'Roach,' I call out, 'any water in your bottle? If so, give this fellow some.' He drinks the bottle dry and is profuse to Roach in his thanks. Might he stay with me he asks! 'You will be safer behind, old cock,' I say. No, he would like to stay! 'Take him to the dugout, Roach,' I say, 'give him some food and let him sleep – he tells me he hasn't slept for ten days on account of the shelling.' The old sailor and the ex-German waiter walk along together, comparing notes and talking of England. Suddenly there is a cloud of smoke, a deafening roar – exit Roach and the unknown German soldier, killed by a German shell.

At that moment a strong rabble of tired, hungry, and thirsty stragglers approach me from the east. I go out to meet them. 'Where are you going?' I ask. One says one thing, one another. They are marched to the water reserve, given a drink and hunted back to fight. Another more formidable party cuts across to the south. They mean business. They are damned if they are going to stay, it's all up. A young sprinting subaltern heads them off. They push by him. He draws his revolver and threatens them. They take no notice. He fires. Down drops a British soldier at his feet. The effect is instantaneous. They turn back to the assistance of their comrades in distress. It is now late afternoon. Most of my officers are dead and wounded. I send for twelve more who have been held in reserve, to swell the corpse roll. Other reinforcements arrive only to be thrown into the melting pot for a similar result. The Germans launch an overwhelming counter-attack which proves successful. They win – to suffer later. At 10 p.m. the curtain rings down on hell. The cost? Enormous. I have seventy men left, all told, out of seven hundred. George Gaffikin is dead; Campbell too has passed on, and when I hear his name I remember his letter still in my pocket. 'I must write a line with it,' I remark to my adjutant. My dugout door that night is like the entrance to a mad-house. One by one wounded officers and men are carried into the trench. McKee, a bright lad, is practically delirious, shot through the lung he still walks and talks. He has lain out in the broiling sun all day. I give him a brandy and soda for which he gives me abuse. We shove him off as soon as we can. Montgomery comes in torn, tattered, filthy and worn out, with wound on head and dent in helmet; him

A BATTLE MESSAGE FROM THE AUTHOR TO MAJOR P. J. WOODS,
9TH ROYAL IRISH RIFLES, THIEPVAL, JULY 2ND, 1916

too we push off after light refreshment. Robbins, a smart youngster, is carried in by two soldiers who are themselves badly wounded, his shrieks can be heard hundreds of yards away, for the firing has now ceased, both sides being exhausted. His leg is fractured below the knee, and he will probably lose it. I try to sleep, but the reaction is too great. I smoke instead, and meanwhile day dawns. The birds have gone, nature has been supplanted. The wood itself has disappeared; was ever there such a day? Not in my recollection. The cavalry are busy all night bringing in the wounded from places which had not been reoccupied by the enemy, and I go out to no man's land, and the first German line, to see about the evacuation of the wounded. About seven hundred dead and wounded lie around in an area of perhaps a quarter of a mile square. Going to the left I am suddenly challenged by a German sentry. I pull out my revolver, fire and miss him; but my orderly, who is behind me, sums up the situation and fires a Very light pistol he is carrying, hitting the Boche in the head and blowing it off. There is another German behind who puts up his hands and shouts 'Kamerad.' The dark is lit up by the burning German whose uniform is on fire. We can take no chances, so I kill the other German with my second round. Then all is quiet and we steal away. We have been in a hornets' nest! The dead can wait, they cannot be nursed back to fighting fitness. I am ordered, at midday, to organise a minor operation. This is a triumph, as I am the junior colonel of the brigade! We lose more men while I gain in reputation! By the morning of the third day I am permitted to withdraw to Martinsart, dazed, but automatic. *My* star is high, even though the sufferings of others are great. A young officer, having fled from the line, is found asleep in the village. Is he to be court martialled? I investigate the matter. No court would find him guilty; not because he did not fly from danger in despair, but because all the men who were with him are dead and cannot give their evidence. So he goes home to Ireland, no longer as a soldier, but as an 'officer resigned,' where he enters business and makes a fortune! Such is a reward for spineless behaviour on the battlefield. War is a contradiction. The fighters seldom come out best, save in this, they keep their souls intact. And that is a possession which no man can take from them.

The net result of the barren, glorious bloody battle of Thiepval is that over seven hundred men of the West Belfast battalion of the Royal Irish Rifles prove their ability to subordinate matter to mind. Intellectual discipline had triumphed.

# CHAPTER V

## REBUILDING AFTER BATTLE

A BATTALION is never really a first-class machine in a great war until it has passed the acid test of big battle with success. At the beginning of the 1914 struggle, regular regiments, fortified by their long tradition and strengthened by their efficiency, met the outburst at Mons with confidence; but even before the war there were units of the regular army which were quite wrongly and unfairly regarded as 'not up to much,' merely because they had not picked up laurels on the field of gore, or killed as many opponents as was considered necessary.

The acid test of killing and being killed had been passed by us with credit. What remained? The memories, the confidence, and seventy men to carry on the torch. It is a peculiar thing that with those assets and the requisite number of reinforcing drafts a unit can be built up again to be quite as good as the defunct organisation, and can be trained in the lethal art to the satisfaction of the most bloodthirsty mercenary yet born. Who knows but that the departed warriors of the old brigade, victors and vanquished alike, may not look down in unison from some other sphere, with approval, as they see the new recruits being trained to cut each others' throats, as was their own fate? Or may it be that from their enhanced position they regard the blood-lust syllabus as a wicked creation of mankind? Who knows, indeed? But for me, as I march out at the head of the small surviving band, that kind of thought I rigorously exclude. War has no room for it. Having trained seven hundred men to kill or incapacitate at least an equal number before 'going west' themselves, my mere duty is to do the same again in a shorter time. All other thoughts I banish: it is the only way. The world in times of Armageddon has no use for aught save killing. Moreover is not the responsibility for the original upheaval jointly mine? Was I not one of the consenting parties to the gamble? Did I not, with Germans and Japanese, Russians and Gallicians and the other 'civilized' countries of the earth consent to the race in armaments? I know we seek shelter behind governmental control, and blame 'the machine' for what we do; but who makes the various 'machines' which plunge us to disaster? Man makes war possible, man can make war unthinkable!

We march along for miles and miles on this

July morn seeking an allotted place whereon to remake our bloody proficiency while, on the other side of the hill, not far off, the Germans are doing precisely the same! Mullins, my orderly, wearing the gilded helmet of a dead Prussian officer, as he walks behind me singing like mad, cracking jokes or making ribald gibes at the expense of Fritz, thinks himself the first man in France today; while Fritz, perhaps wearing the khaki-covered steel helmet of George Gaffikin or Campbell, with beautifully embroidered regimental badge – the gift of some ladies of Belfast – does precisely the same! We have saved the band and bandsmen, old Newton saw to that; does he not know that those same drums will once more have to beat up the Hymn of Hate, and help the weary survivors of that Hate along many a hard road for many a long year, until sheer exhaustion calls a halt? Is it to be only a halt? or shall the 'dismiss' be sounded?

It is the third day of the march back, and we are still seventy strong. We take tickets for all at a local theatre run by a troupe from the Army Service Corps. The brigadier and his staff join us. We just fill the tiny hall. 'Couldn't have done this four days ago, Sir'; says Crowther, a cheery survivor of the reinforcing gang of the second day of the fight, aged eighteen, whose name is soon to appear in the list of immediate awards. He has got blood-lust badly!

He is joking over the dead and destroyed seven hundred whose exit has made it possible for us to give free tickets to seventy, of whom he is one! He doesn't mean to be nasty, of course. He is merely flushed with success! 'Everybody's doing it,' is his and Fritz's justification, which is, in fact, the only justification for war itself, in the eyes of a war fanned population.

We are, the general tells us, to stay at this spot for a few days, and then proceed north by train. 'Train,' says Lightfoot, a novice to us, but not to war itself, 'what a treat!' We take advantage of the pause to reorganise.

'All survivors,' I order, 'will be instructed in the use of the Lewis gun.' The L.G. is more powerful for the purpose of killing than is the rifle, and men are scarce, reinforcements not having yet arrived.

Finding the letter written by Campbell, I address a green envelope to the same address. The letter is to a lady. I write a few lines to explain the circumstances in which the letter came into my possession, and to say her friend died twelve hours after writing to her, like 'a very gallant gentleman.'

The pause is pleasant. Next morning, before the rest are up, as I have given orders for a late lie-in for all, I go to the orderly room alone, to write the story of the epic, for official use, by the aid of messages and reports. I think I am alone. Do my eyes deceive me? Did I see something move underneath the heap of blankets in the corner? I go and look. Lifting up the blanket I see the sleeping figure of a soldier. It is Kelly. Kelly, who endured the preliminary bombardment in the deep dugout for a week amidst the dead and dying; Kelly, who carried messages for three whole days under fire as if with a charmed life. I let him sleep on. In normal times his duty is to clean the orderly room, hence his presence in the *sanctum sanctorum*. At 11 a.m., I am dispensing justice, in the same room, when suddenly, from underneath the blankets emerges the face of Kelly, red, round and flushed. He sizes up the situation and lies low. None else has seen him, as the 'important people' – the sergeant-major, escort, prisoner and witnesses are facing me. I say nothing. At 1 p.m. the office closes. All go to feed. I stay on, saying I am busy and wish to be alone. Still underneath the blankets is Kelly. I call his name and up he jumps in surprise. 'How are you, Kelly?' I ask. He looks sheepish! 'There is nothing to worry about,' I say. He comes to the table. 'How did you know I was there, Sur?' he asks with candour. 'Don't you know, Kelly,' I say, 'it is my business to know everything that goes on in this battalion?' 'That's right, Sur,' he says. 'Well,' I continue, 'tell me all about it?' 'It's like this, Sur,' says the burly Irishman, 'I had hell for ten days in Thiepval, Sur, and when I comes out says I to meself says I: Kelly! at the first long halt you're going to get as drunk as ye darned well can to celebrate your emancipation, an' I did it last night.' 'I see,' I say, 'but do you know what the word emancipation means?' 'No, Sur, not exactly,' he replies, 'but it's a good word, Sur, isn't it?' he asks quite seriously. 'Well, Kelly,' I say, 'you did damned well during the show. I advise you to go and have something to eat – I shall.' We part.

Our officers are almost all new. They require a great deal of attention. Most of them are fresh from home. I warn them about the risk of venereal and the medical officer lectures to them on the same subject, for there is always an inclination on the part of the ladies to bestow their favours on the returned warriors, and the girls of this country-town are no exception to the rule! The lads, fresh from London and elsewhere (Ulstermen, alas! are nearly all used up) reap the benefits bestowed on the few survivors and participate in the freely offered enjoyment which has as its age-old precedent – the reward of valour. 'None but the brave deserve the fair.'

At length we march on to railhead, and there pick up fresh drafts. Montgomery has rejoined me, which is a great relief, despite the fact that he might well have 'wangled' home – for which, in addition to his heroism on 'the day,' he receives the D.S.O.

Tom Foy and Jimmy Law come back to the fold for a time, to help, on the express understanding that they rejoin the general at an early date. As the train is about to depart it is reported that two officers are absent. The engine whistles, the French guard becomes excited. I forbid the guard to start without the missing men. At last they arrive and are pulled into our carriage as the train is on the move. 'What have you got in those packs?' I ask for fun. They both blush! 'Let's have a kit inspection,' I suggest. It is agreed. They 'show kit,' on a carriage seat. The result is astounding! Two pairs of girls' garters and an odd one. Two pairs of silk stockings and a chemise, one nightdress and a string of beads. A pot of vaseline, a candle, two boxes of matches, and an envelope full of astonishing picture postcards, completes the list. 'Souvenirs,' says one rascal. '*Tout prêt*,' says the other.

We go into the trenches again in a quiet sector, nearly opposite Messines. The surroundings are distinctly pleasant, and the weather is good. Our headquarters, when in the line, are actually in a farmhouse, free from enemy observation and therefore quiet. I can ride my horse up to the very door, and almost walk up to the line, unobserved, without entering the trenches. As my duty is to create morale for the next big show I have unlimited opportunity for carrying out this task.

Training facilities outside the line are good, but the finest training ground of all is in no man's land and the German trenches. It is necessary to obtain identification of German divisions and regiments opposite us, as on this Sir Douglas Haig bases his plans for the battle raging further south. We first master no man's land, without which no effective raid is possible. Patrols go out nightly to report on the German wire and the gaps, and the position of sentries. I crawl about a bit myself in strange places. On receiving one particular report I grow suspicious, for I believe the young officer who made it is inventing stories to please me. I know the neutral ground better than he does, but he does not know that. So I tell him I will accompany him to see this strange and useful gap in the German wire about which he writes. We start out after dark, just he and I alone. Crouching, we make for a shallow ditch in which to wait and listen. It will not do to bump into a fighting patrol, as we are weak, yet in our secrecy lies our strength. We crawl as I used to do in the Highlands when stalking the stags and hinds. Halfway between us and the German wire a Very light goes up. The whole land is illuminated for yards around. We throw ourselves flat and look. All's clear on the western front. The light dies down. We advance. We are steering towards the alleged gap. At last we reach the wire. Another Very light

goes up. The figure of a German sentry is sil-
houetted against the dark background of the sky,
not twenty yards off. We pause. 'It is as well I have
given Army some instruction in this sort of thing,'
I think, 'otherwise we would be for it.' The sentry
coughs. 'He has a cold, poor chap,' I muse, 'the
blockade makes his lot less cheerful. Paper shirts
are not much good. Thank God for the Navy!'
The light dies down. We crawl on. 'Hark! what's
this?' I whisper to Army, who is now beside me.
We stop and listen. 'A German relief for that
sentry,' I say in whispering tones, as the beat of
footsteps in unison approaches over the trench
boards. We hug the earth. All is again quiet.
Another Very light goes up. I scan the wire – I am
just opposite the sentry. The light dies down.
I take a ball of twine out of my pocket and tie the
end to a screw stake, leaving the ball there for
future use. We crawl on. Army is getting anxious.
He cannot find his gap. I know he can't; because it
does not exist! We keep up the farce for three hours
and then, pulling Army by the arm, I creep back to
the small ditch halfway across no man's land, in
order that we may speak in whispers. As none of
our patrols are out, any movement must be a hostile
one. I get my face close to Army's and talk to him
in low tones. 'You know where the sentry was,'
I say; 'I tied a ball of string to the wire there. I am

going back to get it and to pay it out across no man's land as I go back. If it's not quite long enough I shall join it to another. You must keep with me, otherwise there may be confusion, as we must both go into our line together at the same place, our sentries will shoot if not.' We proceed on hands and knees until the crawl is necessary. I secure the string and make my way back to the line. The string is not nearly long enough, for we have to return obliquely in order to get in at our prearranged place; but I tie another ball to it and all is well. Once inside the line the task is easy. I walk along the fire steps towards the right, holding the string and winding up all the time, for the distance between me and the German sentry becomes less and less as I go south. Directly I find I have to pay out string again, as I go along, I know I am directly opposite the German sentry. I now secure the string to our parapet. Such a device is only possible from inside our trenches when the parapet is a good deal above the wire, but there are other adaptations to meet other cases.

The hour for stand-to has approached. The men fall in, routine is carried on and rum is issued, while I plot off the right angle to the German sentry from the numbered bay on my trench map. I ask Army to come to breakfast with me. On the way the boy asks me if I think the rum ration is a good thing.

'You're asking me a big question,' I answer laughingly. 'Rum properly issued, under supervision, tot at a time to each, an officer being responsible for the issue, which must be in his presence, no man forced to take it against his wish, no pooling of tots being put into the tea brew, each tot being drunk when issued, in the presence of an officer, is a medicine, ordered only by the divisional commander on the advice of his principal medical officer. It is a temporary restorative in times of great stress. Where the harm comes in is where the regulations concerning the issue of rum are not obeyed, or when youngsters get the taste for strong drink by first drinking rum as a matter of routine and so acquiring the habit of it. The best thing, really, would be for the doctors to discover a better restorative if they can which is not alcoholic, and better still abolish war ourselves and thus do away with the cause which creates the effect. Misguided people at home have, I know, scandalised the army by saying we dope men with rum to make them attack. Such utterances are utterly unworthy of the British race and a slander on our men.'

Breakfast over, I ask Army to come to my room. 'Now look here,' I say, 'I went out on patrol with you for two reasons last night. First to teach you a lesson; secondly to reconnoitre for my own satisfaction. I hope I have succeeded in the first task;

I know I have in the second. You reported a gap which never existed. Had I used your information unchecked dozens of your comrades might have lost their lives on a raid. That they didn't is not your fault. Never do such a thing again. You see the point?' Army is very crestfallen and penitent, so I tell him to forget all – save the lesson. On leaving me to return to his company the boy hesitates to speak but eventually says 'May I go on patrol to-night, Sir, to bring back specific information; I should like to convince you of my reliability?' 'It is a matter for your company commander,' I reply; 'ask him, and if he says "yes," bring in a sample of wire from the horseshoe.' He goes away delighted. Next morning's casualty report from 'A' company shows Army missing. Now I have long ceased to put any value on life in war, and particularly this war, save when life is thrown away. I am not upset over the fact that Army is missing; but I have qualms lest our identity as a regiment has been discovered. True, no badges, papers or discs are taken on patrol but, although the thumb-screw has long since ceased to play its part in the extraction of wanted information, the intelligence departments of the world have their modern methods whereby the truth can be rung out of unwilling prisoners. Starvation, thirst, the placing of hard-boiled eggs in the armpit, threats and such like, all have their places in the practices of war, not written or defined, perhaps, but still there. And why not? Is there much difference between maiming a baby for life in Bloomsbury or Berlin, for no apparent purpose, save the destruction of a locality; and the temporary discomfiture of a combatant in order that the commander-in-chief may be supplied with information, of a most important character, the possession of which may spell life or death to his country? I think the mutilation of the combatant is much more justifiable in theory and supportable in practice! I have no fear of Army splitting on us if unmolested, but few men are impervious to the Intelligence Service, if it is really bent on getting what it wants.

Army I find went out on patrol, left his men lying down and crawled forward to the horseshoe. There was a good deal of stray night firing at the time and no unusual sound was heard. He simply disappeared. Nine months later, when the Second Army launched its successful attack at Messines, over the very spot where Army fell, his skeleton and watch were found in a lonely furrow, near the horseshoe – for good luck, perhaps! He had died for more than a bit of wire. He had saved his soul.

Our plans are now complete for carrying out at least three raids. The whole of the German trench system is known. The wire is cut by the artillery in many places. We have the initiative.

All raids are very much alike. Each man knows his part. As we only require one prisoner on each occasion, and as more are a nuisance, all other enemy soldiers encountered must be put to death. What are our weapons? The pistol, the rifle, the bullet, the bayonet, knuckle-dusters, hook knives with which to rip up, daggers for the heart, butchers' knives for the throat, the bomb for random work, once the prisoner has been extracted and bags of aminal thrown into the dugouts, served up with time fuses, to blow whole companies to smithereens. Tear gas bombs to cause temporary blindness, egg bombs charged with deadly poison to pulverise the lungs and stop the breathing complete the outfit. We moderns are extraordinarily unkind to each other in war – and in peace!

On each raid one prisoner is brought back, while many Germans die, our losses being *nil*. These three successful raids, on the top of the Thiepval epic, stimulate the battalion to such an extent as to place it on the very topmost rung of the war-ladder. Prisoners, trophies and blood are the only true producers of that strange wild mentality which is necessary for war.

During these hectic days I receive the prisoners personally, the number of the regiments concerned being telephoned to G.H.Q., *via* my report centre actually from the German lines. Poor, scraggy, miserable little creatures, glad to be 'free,' thankful to be saved, half-starved and unused to luxuries such as bread and bully beef, they eat ravenously. All prisoners are well fed – at first – because it makes them talk or, at least, revives the long lost tastes, as later it may be necessary to consider withholding the princely fare for purposes of extraction.

What with these raids and trench tours, we are not idle. Apart from training in the field there is the convivial association between the gunners and ourselves to be kept up, while, in Bailleul, the social and recreational centre, later to be reduced to ashes, we dine and wine at regular intervals, *en masse*. The more personal and private revels are not left out. It is not reasonable to expect the youngsters to keep the trenches for England intact, and their chastity inviolable at one and the same time. He who hopes to wage war without wine and women is living in a fool's paradise, for there are no half-measures in war, try how one will.

While in the neighbourhood of Bailleul, despite the greatest care, our 'other rank' casualties from venereal give greater cause for anxiety than our losses in the line. At last we catch the culprit – an infected girl who hops from camp to camp and ditch to dyke like the true butterfly that she is. Then all is well. The officers are better off. Comparative luxury, knowledge and armour stands them in good stead. It is one thing sleeping the night in Lina's arms, after a not too good dinner and minding one's p's and q's: it is another making the best of it in a thorny ditch and standing in a queue later at the Red Lamp clinic where sterilisation is practised. As there are in the ranks of the British Army some of the finest middle- and lower middle-class stock in the Kingdom it is not surprising that young men find themselves in this strange queue, who would, in times of peace, have hesitated to line up outside a music hall.

How have the mighty fallen! But as the mighty hold equal blame with the opportunists for the presence of war in our midst, they can hardly complain when their sons – and daughters, are bitten!

At this period I am seriously exercised in my mind owing to the behaviour of two battalion commanders on whom I am forced to rely to a great extent for co-operation, and to whom the safety of the line is of less importance than the whisky bottle. Both are cheery amiable fellows in the ordinary way, but our present way is no ordinary way. Both are of that pre-war type – good mess presidents and judges of wine – but both are now a menace to our safety. One has just kept me waiting several hours after the relief of the line was complete, during which period I commanded his battalion in action, while he was finishing his port in billets! The other had become so drunk during a relief of the line that the outgoing colonel refused to hand over to him, and remained on in command of the toper's men until he had slept off his liquor. My interest in this latter case is chiefly centred in the menace to my flank.

I decide to see a staff officer, quietly, about this delicate matter: with the result that later on a change of scenery is arranged for the two tipplers. Although both were awarded the D.S.O., as a solace to their souls, yet their removal to realms of comfort at home strengthened the line, but undoubtedly weakened the home front and jeopardised the lives of youngsters.

I had not long previously been forced to call the attention of a brigade commander of a formation with which I had cause to be remotely connected, from time to time, to a most extraordinary sight I had witnessed. To my amazement I saw a colonel sitting at the entrance to a communication trench, personally issuing unauthorised tots of rum to his men as they passed him in single file at 3 p.m., on a fine clear Spring-like afternoon, on their way to hold a line for the very first time. The brigadier did not seem to realise the gravity of the case. He did not appreciate the danger. The mentality of this colonel was all wrong. Badly based on brandy, he thought everybody else felt as he did – dejected and desolate. Despondent and at all times *difficile*, he was a victim of drugs and drink, and ultimately died. But, and here is the important point, because he had local pull, he had been entrusted with the care of youth for eighteen months. This was bad enough. The safety of the line was another matter. Seeing what I had seen, knowing what I knew and visualising the future, as his brigadier took no notice of my protest, even going so far as to say the matter was no business of mine, I determined on having the wretchedly miserable man removed, for the good of us all. I saw a very senior medical officer about the matter and persuaded him to take action, with the result that the drink-drug addict was removed to England, there to degenerate and eventually die. The safety of the line outweighed all other considerations. Drink control was imperative.

I sit at tea, in the line, when the telephone rings. I go to it as I am wanted. I am told I am promoted brigadier-general, and that I must proceed next day to my new command on the Somme. I go round the Royal Irish Rifles line for the last time, at once, to say *au revoir*.

The curtain rings down on this portion of the stage. 'Keep the flag flying,' I tell them. 'There's no German like a dead German,' I enjoin. I don't believe it, but it goes down! Fifteen months of successful blood and thunder is over, but much more lies ahead.

# CHAPTER VI

## NEW MEN—OLD METHODS

As I leave my divisional commander, General Nugent, a fine fellow, who has particularly asked to see me, to say 'Good-bye,' he gives me a bit of sound advice which I always hold in front of me. 'Treat your new brigade like a big battalion,' he says. Some did not like General Nugent! The reason was not hard to seek! He was a very fine soldier! His staff swore by him, and that is enough. Now he has passed on to the great majority, like so many war leaders, a victim, no doubt of the aftermath, brought about by the strain of service in the Empire's cause,

Napoleon once said there were no bad soldiers, only bad colonels, which perhaps accounts for the introduction I have to my new command. I present myself to my new divisional headquarters. The division is at rest near Abbeville. It is new to France. The men have been in the line for a short period. 'I'm afraid you'll be disappointed with your new command,' I am told. I start to think. Why should I be disappointed? I think to myself and then I ask,

'How long have they been in this Division?' 'Oh, about two years,' is the reply. 'And you?' I add enquiringly. 'The same,' is the unexpected answer I receive. I think still harder.

During the next week, on the march, I take stock. The men are good. They are Celtic Bantams, from Wales. I am used to Celts.

'Treat your new brigade like a big battalion,' rings in my ears, the words of General Nugent.

Starrett, my servant, and McKinstry the groom have come with me. A week after arrival, when stationary, I ask Starrett when dressing, 'What do you think of this lot?' 'They'll be all right presently,' he replies. I say no more.

We have a monster kit inspection. 'Is it necessary for you to see all the battalions and the rest, at the same time? It is *most* inconvenient' says a staff officer. 'Yes,' I say, 'it is not inconvenient for me, and men and battalions sometimes swap kits!' That staff officer changed his job.

We receive orders to go into the line on the right of the British Army, near the River Somme. The great battle of 1916 has died down. It is November. The weather has brought the fight to a standstill. 'General Winter' is in command. We occupy a line recently taken over from the French. In reality there is no line in the trench sense. The men occupy shellholes. Six entire villages in the neighbourhood have been destroyed by the shells of both sides. Only a little red rubble remains, and that is mostly brick mud. It freezes hard, then it thaws. Never was there a winter such as the men endured in 1916 and 1917. The last was bad enough; this is worse, as accommodation in the line does not exist. Dugouts and communication trenches cannot be constructed during a battle; after, it is too late, as the mud and rain prevent the carrying up of material. Latrines there are none. The sanitary arrangements are entirely haphazard and makeshift. Disinfectants help. We at brigade are comfortable – the French have seen to that. Otherwise the conditions are appalling. The condition known as trench feet is our bugbear; but the measures taken last year, if properly carried out, suffice to combat the evil. One battalion, through neglect, loses over a hundred men in four days from this malady. The colonel is at fault, and goes away. This example improves matters.

Little can be done, except keep the sick rate down during the next three trying months. How the men live I do not know. They cannot be reached by day as there are no trenches. Cover there is none. Once this place was a field of corn, now it is a sea of mud. On it the French fought a desperate battle, earlier in the year. My daily route on a duckboard track lies through the Rancourt valley. I count a hundred and two unburied Frenchmen, lying as they fell, to the left of me; while opposite there are the corpses of fifty-five German machine-gunners by their guns, the cartridge belts and boxes still being in position. Viewed from the technical and tactical point of view their dead bodies and the machine guns afford a first-rate exposition of modern tactics. Later, when the ground hardens, and we can walk about without fear of drowning or being engulfed, I take officers over the battlefield and point out the lessons to be learnt, having in view the positions of the dead bodies. The stench is awful; but then, and only then, are we able to get at the dead for burial. If the times are hard for human beings, on account of the mud and misery which they endure with astounding fortitude, the same may be said of the animals. My heart bleeds for the horses and mules. We are in the wilderness, miles from towns and theatres, the flood of battle having parched the hills and dales of Picardy in its advance against civilization. Like all other floods, it carries disaster in its track, with this addition, being man-made, and ill-founded, as it is, in its primary inception, it lacks the lustre of God-inspired help. God is wrongly claimed as an ally, by both parties, to the detriment of the other; whereas the Almighty, benevolent and magnanimous, watches over all and waits the call to enter – but not as a destroyer.

The men in muddy hell need daily supplies. The conditions are so vile that no man can endure more than forty-eight hours at a stretch in the forward puddles and squelch pits. Do those at home in comfort, warmth, and cultured environment realise what they owe to the stout hearts on the western front? No wheeled traffic can approach within three miles of the forward pits; for roads which were useful to the pre-war farmers have now disappeared. Everything must be carried up by men or mules. The latter, stripped of harness, or fully dressed, die nightly in the holes and craters, as they bring their loads to the men they serve so faithfully and well, urged on by whips and kindness. But one false step means death by suffocation. Sheer exhaustion claims its quota, for the transport lines themselves are devoid of cover from wind and rain. Such is the animals' war, and could animal lovers see the distress of their dumb friends they would never permit another conflict.

A trivial incident sticks in my mind as I write, and recalls the abnormality of our war lives and minds. An old French ammunition dump exploded as I passed, killing many Welshmen, two German prisoners, and a French salvage worker. A German shell had hit the dump. 'What an international party,' I exclaimed, as I helped to sift out the dead from the dying, 'twelve Welshmen, two Germans and a Frenchman.' 'The proportion is not good,' answered a staff officer seriously.

As a brigade we are relieved every eighth night, the exhausted men being lorried back to cold hutments, in the midst of the same sea of squalour at Bray. No wonder when men go on leave they fall prey to every kind of evil in order to forget ! But I have one important factor less to deal with than is usual. I cannot be attacked. I am in a muddy wilderness and between the enemy and me is a muddy barrier over which organised advance is impossible. I need no wire and even if I did I cannot get it there. The men carry two days' food on their backs, as they go in – to save the mules; but there is a limit to the strength of even a Welsh miner. True, marauding hostile patrols occasionally penetrate for information, but they can do little harm. True, I lose a good colonel, stabbed in three places and shot in two, by a German sergeant who, having lost his way, sees his chance; but I cannot have wire on my front – the mud prevents it. I receive a message saying the corps commander will hold a conference in my dugout. Mahomet has to come to the mountain of mud. At eleven o'clock the big bugs arrive. Generals of all kinds and grades approach. The conference starts. The subject is wiring of the front line. I see my work report on the table. 'Wiring – *nil*,' I read at a distance.

'How much wire have you put out, Crozier?' asks the lieutenant-general, a goodly man whom I like and from whom I am subsequently to receive much kindness. 'None, Sir,' I answer up quickly. 'Why?' is the next interrogation I receive. 'For two reasons, Sir,' I answer; 'firstly, I cannot get wire up to the pits and shellholes, secondly, no one can attack me over the mud if I can't attack them.' 'Have you no wire at all out?' I am further asked. 'Only that, Sir, which was put out when the ground was dry, before we came in, and one long strand of barbed wire between each post, fifteen hundred yards in all,' I reply. 'What's the good of one strand of barbed wire?' he asks. 'To keep me and others from walking over to the German lines by mistake!' I reply. There is a pause – then a laugh – the situation is saved.

'The division on your right has put out a great deal of wire: here's their report,' says the corps commander. I read and pass it back. 'What have you to say to that?' he asks, not unkindly. 'I don't know anything about that front, Sir,' I discreetly reply, 'but it is neither feasible nor necessary here.' 'Well,' he says, 'do what you can.'

The conference ends in gas, as such things sometimes do.

It is fatal to imagine that wire has been put out and then to report that it has! The day inevitably arrives when, for some cause or other, the wire is looked for, under more advantageous conditions, and is found 'absent without leave!'

Three months later, when the Germans retired to the Hindenburg line, we were holding the 'much wired front of the division on the right'. It became our duty not only to pursue, but to report back the first signs of enemy withdrawal. My staff did so in these words: 'The enemy has made an orderly and systematic withdrawal along the whole of our front. Evidently he is short of wire as he has pulled up all in front of his own line, and ours, and taken it away!' We had lost many things in the mud and mire, but our sense of humour was never lacking.

At last the sun begins to shine. Spring peeps through the mist which rises from that which is now probably the best known river in the world – the Somme. The river runs through my front: on the right are the French. I shoot quantities of duck in the marshes for the mess and company cooks to deal with, and take some over to the French general. He is delighted. I ask a favour. I want to seize a small hill on my right front which is giving me trouble. The Boches snipe from there at long range, and observe their artillery fire on to our line with ease. It is only a mound and isolated. 'Will you help me, by co-operating on your front?' I ask. 'Useless,' he replies, throwing up his hands; 'they will go shortly,' he adds. I persist. He shakes his old grey head! 'No, no, I can,' he says; 'but you will lose much, I little, it is not worth it; if I help you, you will suffer. You can't move without me. I don't move, you don't suffer!' ' Well, *Mon Général*.' I reply, 'I shall attack without warning, and if I don't take it, I will eat my hat!' He roars with laughter. He has never heard of such a thing! A British general eating his hat! 'Which one,' he asks, 'the tin one or the *chic* one?' 'The *chic* one,' I reply; 'and if I win you eat the tin one!' We part great friends. Now I have good reasons for wanting to take the little mound, apart altogether from the sniping and observation. I have formed a very high opinion of the calibre of the men and their officers. The staff has been renovated, and their methods and military mentality have been improved. I have eaten the leek with each of the Welch battalions on St. David's Day, and know their outlook on the 'bloody problem' to be the right one. They have been starved of help, support, backing and example. No men could have come through the muddy, pestilential hell of the winter with hearts unbroken unless those hearts were in the right places. We now have new colonels, majors, adjutants, doctors, transport officers, and quartermasters. These are all in a vice grip. All that is now requisite is an initial minor success of our own, unplanned by outsiders, aided by none other than our own gunners, and carried out with dash. The little men will do it! They can get *their* hill! Their tails can be up, never to come down. That is why I want the mound. I talk to them all and let them into the spoof-secret. There is nothing like a good family secret, in war: it makes the family. They get their hill with practically no loss, and the 119th (Welch) Brigade is made for ever. The old French general is delighted, and telegraphs: '*Bravo! Monsieur le Général ne mangera pas son chapeau, mais il m'excusera?*'

My day comes, St. Patrick's Day; for Irish soldiers are allowed to wear the shamrock in memory of Irish heroism in South Africa. There they bought 'the gesture' with their blood, for which Irish soldiers had gone to the cells for years! I am not alone, as I have Starrett and McKinstry with me and the Rifle cap badge and orange tabs, to show the way, and act as the torch. The spirit of George Gaffikin has entered into the souls of misjudged Welshmen – we – Starrett, McKinstry and I are here, earthly representatives of the departed 9th Rifles.

On St. Patrick's Day, although the weather is still vile, as the rain has turned the ground into mud again, the South Wales Borderers enter the German lines by force, and, having thrown some bombs, report the position only lightly held. Two days later the enemy is in ordered retreat.

We follow as best we can. Roads are only partially useful, as road junctions have been cratered, and the deliberate devastation of the countryside is dreadful to behold. Houses have been blown up, and, where that has not been possible, roofs have been blown off. Fruit trees have been irreparably damaged and farm produce has been laid waste. The civilian population has been marched to bondage in a foreign land to work in its enemy's cause. Destruction, such as Napoleon never contemplated, lies before us, a visible sign of the tragedy and futility of modern war.

Peronne, the ancient town in which the Duke of Burgundy, in 1468, forced Louis XI to sign a treaty recognising his independence, is a shambles. Equancourt, Etricourt and other neighbouring villages are no better.

The Indian Cavalry come up, in hope of mounted action, and wallow in the mud, famished with cold, and entirely out of their element. What must they think of the barbarous action of western culture, in laying waste the countryside? Perhaps they are not surprised, for has not war been part and parcel of their own destiny since time immemorial?

The little Welsh miners prove themselves splendid workers on the roads which they repair, by filling the craters at road junctions, with the brick and rubble of the exiled Frenchmen's homes. Is it not a case of earth to earth and ashes to ashes? The French soil eats up the homes of Frenchmen, thanks to the prevalent ideas of might and right!

On April 21st and 24th, and again in May, the Welshmen prove their mettle in open fighting. The Borderers take XV. Ravine, the Welch the ridge named after them, while the Royal Welch plant their bayonets in front of La Vacquerie and call the place Fusilier Ridge. The men are splendid.

They enter La Vacquerie itself for a game of tip and run, damaging dugouts and killing Germans. Andrews, a Scot, in August, 1914 a private, now a major, M.C., and shortly to be a colonel, wins the D.S.O. There is no holding these intrepid men from the Principality, of whom it was said six months ago 'they are no good.'

We pause, and as we glare at our enemy, well dug in on the Hindenburg line, a thousand yards or more away, we realise we have vast unthought-of opportunity for making ourselves into a fighting formation, equal to the best in France today.

Although the fighting has been insignificant, in comparison with the bloody carnage of the Somme, we have lost as many officers and men as would in former days have sent their commander, *dégommé* to Stellenbosch, during the Boer War.

Colonel Pope, the commanding officer of the Borderers, becomes a casualty. Tripping over some

GERMAN PRISONERS TAKEN BY 119TH INFANTRY BRIGADE AT LA VACQUERIE, MAY, 1917

rusty wire he falls and punctures his face. Two years later a military funeral leaves Millbank Hospital, and on the gun-carriage are the mortal remains of Pope. The dirty wire killed him.

We are now in country unspoilt by battle, save for a shellhole, here and there. Its turn is to come in six months' time. The woods are green, the partridges are nesting. We salve the hay and clover, and gather mushrooms in the cellars. This seems a heaven-sent opportunity for the men to learn all about war and to be quietly entered before a more gigantic fray.

Minor operations are the order of the day. The Welch bag a machine gun and prisoners on their own initiative; the Fusiliers make a most valuable identification; the Borderers carry out well-planned raids. Meanwhile, in wide no man's land, swept free from Germans, each man learns war-sense, and in the line itself the miners create a model trench system.

Yet even in these pleasant surroundings the tragedy of war is with us.

Two officer patrols of one regiment meet by mistake in no man's land, and, each mistaking the other for an enemy, gets to grips in no uncertain manner, with all the usual implements of destruction and disastrous results in dead and wounded. In hospital, the leader of each patrol tells the other how he 'knocked merry hell out of the Hun!' If proof is ever wanting as to what these little men do, on their own, in the privacy of neutral ground in which they dominate, here is the essence of confirmation!

But I have my troubles. The army does not possess a psychological department, as does any other big concern. Round pegs are shoved into square holes. The old army, which runs the great national army, knows nothing about psychology and cares less. Names, ranks, records, length of service and suchlike things count most. When things and men run right it is purely a matter of luck, because unless the personal factor is taken into account, the formula is incomplete. Personal friendships and ability to tell good stories over a glass of port or to toady to military magnates are made the hidden reasons for recommendations for promotion. I will have none of it. With us it is leadership, the lives of men and victory. That is why I have to send away a colonel, a charming fellow, a staff college graduate and a one-time instructor of some military subject, at some military establishment, sent to me for a month 'to qualify for a brigade.' He is unable to kick the Germans out of his line quickly on his own initiative, and prefers to write orders instead of doing things!

'But you can't do that,' I'm told; 'he has been a G.S.O. and is to command a brigade!' 'And what about the line and the men?' I ask. 'Oh, he'll be all right with a little experience,' is the reply. 'The war has been on nearly three years,' I say; 'and experience is gained here, not in offices, or on staffs: the chief knows that, and says staff officers are to go to battalions to get their promotion to fighting brigades. You seek to evade the order by wringing a recommendation out of me. I have two first-class colonels here, one was a sergeant-major in the Royal Irish Regt. in 1914; the other was a second lieutenant in the Ceylon Planters Corps in the same year. They are both going to be recommended for brigades after the first big show – if they live. See? Now our friend is going on ten days' leave, to make things easier; and in the meantime you can get him another job. We all have our *métiers* and his is neither the command of men nor the slaughtering of the enemy.' They didn't believe me, but he went; and died later – with four hundred other men, the result of a mistake. Four obviously unsuitable, yet recommended as suitable, colonels have to be sent away in four months on account of their psychological unsuitability to take part in the great and ghastly struggle, and their inability to lead men or to hold the line with confidence. 'To recommend such men is a dereliction of duty, a violation of the trust imposed by the King's commission,' I tell the commander-in-chief.

My days are spent crawling about no man's land

in the long grass, sometimes alone, sometimes with my orderly officer. On one of these excursions I crawl to see the wire in front of Gonnelieu by day I am alone, as one crawler makes less rustle than two. Suddenly I reach an isolated shellhole (the ground is little broken) and, peering into it from the grass above, see a German looking up at me. I see his hand go to his pocket. 'He may have a small bomb or pistol,' I think to myself. He starts to move and appears stiff. He may shout, he is within thirty yards of his wire! or shoot! I draw my revolver and jump down on him into the six feet deep hole. He is a big fellow but evidently wounded. I get him by the throat and press the muzzle of the revolver to his chest. 'I'd like his life, in preference to his escape' I think, 'but I want his regimental identification.' I cannot speak German. I hardly know two words. 'Hands up,' I order, in lowered tones. He understands, complies and mutters '*Kamerad*.' I don't trust him, but, pushing the muzzle harder to emphasise its purpose, I search him with my left hand, and gain some papers which I transfer to my pocket. I see no numerals on his clothing. '*Was ist dein Regiment?*' I venture emphatically, giving the muzzle an extra push! He does not answer. He does not wish to divulge. '*Zu komme mit mir,*' I order, pointing to our line. He points to his leg. '*Ich forstein,*' I say. He rises slowly. It is not easy to get out of a big shellhole in any case. I can't help feeling he wishes to come over to us, although he was probably waiting until dusk to crawl into his own lines. I give him a push up behind and clamber up myself alongside of him as he hangs on the lip of the crater, covering him with the revolver as best I can. I roll on my side in the long grass and drag him up to the level ground. I know I am right now, as if he gives the show away, he knows they will loose off at both of us. He crawls beside me for two hundred yards, and then we sit down in a depression in the ground. I start to smile – he follows suit.

'You spoke German?' he asks. I shake my head. 'Me no spoke Englesh,' he replies. We are alone! I look at my watch. It is 12 o'clock. At 1 o'clock an officer is coming to lunch with me as I have to talk to him about a court martial of which he was president. We hurry on. I am afraid of my prisoner being seen first as the Welshmen have a habit of firing first, and getting the identification afterwards! So, as I near my entrance gap, I show myself. The sentry sees me. All is well. I point to the German. The sentry's face beams all over. It is a sweltering day. 'Give this man a drink,' I say to the corporal in charge of the post, 'and send him down to my headquarters as soon as you can, but tell your captain.'

Morton comes to lunch. I hand the Boche papers over to be dealt with, and forget all about my shell-hole companion. There is no time in war for anything save getting on to the next job. At lunch the fare is good. May and Barkey see to that, and the port is popular. I take Morton to my tin shanty. Morton has been an agent to some duke or lord. He is quite a good fellow; but he has, by fate, been roped into war rather late in life. He is now probably forty and is a major. I like him because he happens to be a gentleman. He is endeavouring to apply humane principles to war and has, when president of a court, allowed a soldier to be sentenced to a mere life sentence of penal servitude, for sleeping on his post when a sentry, despite the fact that the crime is rather prevalent and that at a parade of officers of each battalion I have personally warned all of the danger to the army of sentries sleeping and have explained that the thing to do is to stop it, or if men are tried for it to inflict the maximum penalty of death, which can be commuted, and must be confirmed by the commander-in-chief.

'You must,' I say to Morton, 'Re-orient your mind – you are a senior officer, with responsibilities, taking part in war. Neither you or I can pull our weight unless we behave as "war-dogs." We must be ruthless to be kind, hard to be faithful, humane to be good soldiers when there is room for it, and absolutely just at all times. I told you about the prevalence of this crime. The Army Act protects the prisoner, you have to protect the army – Do you see?' 'No, Sir, I don't,' he says, 'I thought a life sentence sufficient and——' 'I stop him – 'You don't come into it like that,' I tell him, 'you are merely there to do justice, not only to the prisoner but to discipline. It is not for you to judge on the prevalence of a certain crime. I advise the commander-in-chief about that and he views the whole of the Armies in the same respect. Now Morton, I never intended to be hard on you, but cease to think like a land agent, and act like a steel soldier, not a tin one. If you don't you'll have to go. Do you understand? I can't have my discipline upset. Do you wish to say anything more?' 'Yes,' he replies, 'I should like to see the divisional commander.' 'You may, of course,' I answer; 'but don't forget I am only giving you advice which I need never give you. The matter is not urgent. I am going on leave at 6 a.m. tomorrow morning. When I come back I shall arrange for you to see the divisional commander, if you still wish it then. Good-bye. Help yourself to a drink in the mess. I'm busy.' I heard no more of it.

At Munich, at a dinner long after the war, I talked to an ex-Bavarian soldier who had been captured in a raid in 1917. I asked him to describe his experiences when captured. 'We were terrified and surprised,' he said, 'in our dugout. An English soldier threw a small bomb into the dugout. My brother and I and two friends escaped the shock of explosion and made our way up the steep steps. On gaining the trench I was immediately seized from behind and partly stunned by a blow from a club. Some dozen Englishmen with blackened faces surrounded us. I saw my brother fall, stabbed to the heart by a dagger, by a powerful young English officer of tender years. His time was not long and my brother was avenged, as a German sergeant killed him with a pistol shot. The conflict was great but we were overpowered. Your men fought like savages and so did we. They only wanted one prisoner and I was handy, and not too heavy for dragging across to your lines. So they selected me and to that I owe my life. They shot the rest of my comrades, some ten in all, and blew up more in their holes and caves. I struggled to get free, and they knocked me senseless: they would not kill me as I was worth my weight in gold! I could divulge and they knew it! Coming to myself again, I found myself in an English dugout being given water. I was kindly treated – was I not of value as an informer? – and plied with questions, which I said I could not answer, as I knew nothing. I was conducted to a place called Fins where I was again

A GERMAN PRISONER CAPTURED IN 1917

"put through it," but with kindness. They got all they wanted by degrees and cross-examination. They were clever.' I was very much interested in this account of a daring exploit on the part of our men, for it requires nerve to enter the enemy lines in cold blood, and enterprise 'to get away with it;' and as we held the line in front of Fins in 1917, where he was captured, and from what he described and the fact that an officer was killed (they carried his body back with great difficulty), I was convinced my Welshmen and not Englishmen had carried out the raid.

'I believe my men got you,' I said, 'and I was not far off.' 'And my poor brother!' he answered shaking his head sadly. 'They were Welshmen,' I said, 'not Englishmen.' 'They were devils,' he replied, half savagely; 'but there,' he added smilingly, 'all that is over and we are friends as never before,' holding out his hand; 'but,' he added, 'I would still like to get hold of one swine!' 'Who is that?' I asked, in surprise. 'The man who stole my watch!' he replied. 'My life was nothing, it was that of a dog anyhow, a whipped dog, but my watch my mother gave me, and the war and the death of my brother killed her.' Tears came into his eyes. 'And you planned it,' he said simply and half reproachfully, 'you only did your duty!'

Many senior officers did not carry out personal

reconnaissance in close contact with the enemy. I found such absolutely necessary for the drawing up of plans. By 1917 a completely new technique of the line had come into vogue, and only those who used it could hope for success.

Frequent discussions with ex-enemy soldiers in Hungary, Austria, Germany and Czecho-Slovakia confirm the opinion I had formed some time ago, namely, that the propaganda departments and the popular Press of the various countries alone enabled the war to be carried on so long. It is to be hoped that the Press of the world will throw its weight into the scales for permanent peace as readily and efficiently as it did for the purposes of war.

But for all that, in the course of my travels on the Continent, where I have been most hospitably entertained and most kindly received by ex-enemies of all classes, I have never heard any doubt expressed that the peoples of the Associated Powers thought at the outset that they would win the war. But in 1917 they all realised their fate – America sealed it.

But to revert to the year 1917.

I look forward to leave which I now take regularly every three months, as I am working at high pressure. But, out in the not unpleasant wilderness, miles from the nearest inhabited town, I have been able to devote unstinted attention to the fighting machine.

I have preached the lesson of the failure of Spion Kop time after time to all ranks.

The brigade is entirely free from non-military troubles caused by wine and women, owing to the absence of both: save beer as a regulated issue on payment – we have not descended to the rationing of women! Being in the wilderness has its compensations. The men's health is better, and I am spared the necessity of expending energy on futile courts martial and preventive measures. I feel I can now go home for ten days with confidence, as I have succeeded in obtaining four first-class commanding officers – Benzie and Plunkett to whom I have already referred; Andrews, whom I alone, I think, understand and who revels in war for the excitement's sake and is adored by his men; and Kennedy, a Scottish professor. All these men are without frills.

Another bad result of the war had become manifest in the minds of men. Gross extravagance has broken out in all ranks of society at home and in the field. It is with the latter I am concerned. Mere boys of eighteen and upwards, who otherwise would have been at school or the university, or learning some profession or trade, were rushed into commissions, armed with stars, cheque books and authority, and often possessed of a quite erroneous knowledge of the value of money or the value of the things they imagined they had to do to keep up an appearance. Senior officers often set very bad examples in this respect, and this I would not tolerate.

I remember one rich brigadier who in 1916 kept a sort of open mess for which he paid, but which was more like a society lunch than a serious effort to establish war hardness and endurance. Chickens, hams, jellies, wines and various rich and unwholesome foods were posted to this soldier daily by a devoted wife, or consigned from fashionable stores. It was not war. The result was that an entirely false sense of the value of luxuries was fostered throughout the whole *ménage;* and that the succeeding brigadier was placed in a very false position, for he had neither the money to pay for this unwholesome extravagance, nor the desire to do so if he had. He had to build afresh.

The majority of the lads had no idea of control of their banking accounts; their thoughts were rightly on the line, and killing Germans; and when they got away for a spree, they went the whole hog. It was all wrong and unfair on them. Taking every case on its merits, I generally refused to allow a boy-officer to be prosecuted for having his cheques returned, as I felt his position was a false one, and his temptations such as no British boy should be subjected to.

Naturally many boys married in haste, while on

leave, in order to be able to taste the pleasures of life in the open, while the girls underwent the same twists of mind. The financial chaos resulting from a wrong sense of money values, or no sense at all, sometimes made these unions very difficult. In themselves, I held, at the time, that they were inevitable and often good; but the economic factors often caused utter disaster, the results of which are with us today.

It is perfectly clear to me, that in the future, if a rumour of war is ever hushed or noised around, the peoples of the world must all rise up and say 'No,' with no uncertain voice: not because they are now denied any chance of real victory in the field which soldiers have been able to promise with reasonable certainty in the past, prior to 1914 – in that respect, 'the game is up;' but because of the havoc which is created in the ramifications of daily life among the young and innocent. A gamble in war might be excusable if only the players stood to suffer; but no man or nation has a right to gamble on the break-up of the moral fibres of society or of civilisation itself.

But there has now appeared a third factor in the game of war: hitherto there were only two, the puppets of victory and defeat. Now those who arrange the wars and take the initial steps will surely suffer too. This may be our safeguard. The vulnerability of Whitehall and suchlike places of the earth from the air; the certain knowledge on the part of the politicians, statesmen, diplomats, profiteers and wire-pullers (hitherto quite safe) that they will be among the first to die, and the threatened loss of treasure by men of big business, may yet save the honour of our youths and maidens, and stave off the decay of our race; because suffering, to be known and realised, has to be endured or visualised as a certainty. But the 'interested rings' which turn out battleships and munitions will have to be watched and kept in order, as avarice is a 'diehard.' And again, many people were happy in the outbreak of 1914. I was one of them. I am now chastened, as I have seen the suffering. I shall, of course, fight again if I have to, in defence of my country; but I advise other and wiser methods than war for the settling of disputes. I knew, in 1914, that I must either get on or get under. Dug-out officers, more particularly senior ones, welcomed war. To them came power and pay without any danger. Unhappy husbands and miserable wives welcomed war as a way out and even courted death. Munition makers and caterers, clothiers and countless other people welcomed war. There will always be some who put profit before patriotism.

Youth sprang to the call but, thank God, British youth always will, if guided. Let us guide our youth to the hard battle of peace.

All this is now changed. If we are stupid enough to resort again to the last resource of fools, everybody will have to be in it. There will be neither objectors or tribunals, conscience or exemption.

To come back to 1917.

The characteristics of war are now so changed that an officer who was a captain at Mons, and has been at home in a soft job ever since being wounded in 1914, is useless in command of a battalion. I have no time to teach him, neither is it my duty so to do, so we part friends for our common benefit.

It became increasingly difficult, as time went on, to obtain correct reports from officer patrols, as regards information about the enemy line on which to base plans for raids. This was due to the lack of training at home of young officers. My colonel and I had always to verify all reports on wire by personal reconnaissance, which we carried out separately, and which we used to cross-check with each other. It was the only way in which to minimise loss and ensure success. The happenings on these midnight and daylight excursions always brought excitement, novelty and usually success. One such stands out vividly in my mind.

I, with an orderly, had been observing for many nights an enemy sentry in the moonlight, at about twenty yards distance, so as to obtain correct information as to the relief of posts. One night we evidently approached too close, and exploded a warning signal by contact. The whole line suddenly lit up with rifle fire and Very lights, while we lay flat on our faces. At last the excitement subsided and only then had I an opportunity of looking up in the fading moonlight to see a single sentry less than twenty yards from me, staring in my direction, immovable. He was evidently suspicious and probably posted on purpose for our benefit. For two hours he stared. At last I judged that something would have to be done, as daylight was approaching, and if I lay out there much longer we should be seen. I could not speak to the orderly, who lay slightly to my right rear. I also surmised that the sentry would shortly be relieved and his successor perhaps be more vigilant. What was to be done? If I moved back he would see me and fire. Very lights went off every few minutes. I drew my revolver in the moonlight and waited for a Very light to go up, and then I experimented to find out whether I could see the sight or the muzzle. I could see both in the grass in front of me. When the next light went up I tested against the man himself. I decided to fire, when the next light went up. I calculated that even if I missed him he might be astonished and give us a second or two in which to scamper back into cover. I fired. He fell. 'Run like hell,' I said to the orderly, which we both did. A hundred yards away in no man's land was a gravel pit for which we made, to the accompaniment of a sort of Brock's benefit. Into it we jumped and there we lit cigarettes and smoked in comfort until it was time to crawl back to our sap in safety. We left that spot for a month while the local excitement died down, but subsequently raided the post, capturing very valuable identification of a new division.

I go on leave; and on my return to France I spend the night at Boulogne for the purpose of seeing a base echelon in which I am interested. I ask a girl friend, whose father is my neighbour, to dine with me. She is married, but her husband is in Mespot. and she herself is driving a car for some Base bureaucrat. She calls for me at my hotel. 'Where shall we dine?' I ask. She selects Mony's, as the fried sole is excellent there.

During dinner she points me out various girl comrades of hers and to some I am introduced.

They ask me what I am going to do after dinner. 'I know nothing about Boulogne in war time, thank goodness,' I reply. 'What is there to do?' I ask. 'Oh,' says one, 'you can come up to our club room and have a sing-song; but you'll have to leave at 10 o'clock, as they don't trust even generals with us after that.' 'Or you can,' says another to me, 'ask us to your hotel and order drinks for us in a private room, *hôteliers* do anything for generals here!

What do you say, girls? Let's wine with the general, and perhaps if we're good he'll give us supper too!' 'What do you say, Madge?' I ask my friend. 'It would be great fun,' she replies. We make a move to the hotel. On the way down, Madge tells me these girls are all very good sorts, and that they do not go in for lovers and such like. 'This place is now a hotbed of iniquity,' she adds; 'there are some very good sorts here of both sexes, and they all have to work hard, but the morals of many of the men have disappeared, while the girls have become war-mad and sex-mad: in many cases these go together and free love is easy. There are so many rooms they can go to. The war has made me quite frank myself, otherwise I wouldn't talk to you like this,' she says laughingly. 'But don't be afraid – I'm quite safe! Last week three girls and three boys from the line took one room in an hotel, all got drunk, and stayed there some hours. The girls had to be in by ten but they all went to sleep, so the girls were late. There was a row, but nothing came out. I know, because one of the girls whom I know left a purse under her pillow, and I went straight to the room and got it for her! The boys were still in bed. Immorality in Boulogne is as prevalent as death in the line!' 'You do not surprise me in the least,' I say. 'But do you think the dear old ladies at home have any idea of what is going on, or what their daughters are in contact with?' I ask. 'Not in the least,' Madge replies. 'There are thousands of worthy people in the old country who hardly have an idea the war is on, or what it means. Others run hospitals, great and small, because it is the thing to do; others trot off to war-work gaily, and make splints and badges for the broken, as if they were selling programmes at a society matinée! They use the work centres as gas and gossip clubs, and talk over the scandals of society. I know what I'm talking about, because I know four dear old ladies who are well in it – one is very wealthy and does nothing at all, save regard the war as an invention of the devil sent to interfere with her personal routine, while another is honest at heart and does her best on a small scale in the hospital world, but she doesn't grasp the magnitude of the war; the third, being an autocrat of the worst type, sits on committees and loves domineering the rest of her neighbours; while the fourth, a talker, honestly thinks she is doing her bit – that cursed expression – but being an intensely stupid woman is only a hindrance to her fellow workers. But remember, many of the men and women at home are having the time of their lives; only the war victims themselves, personally hurt through the death of their nearest and dearest, really know what war is, and can appreciate the sufferings out here. There are many exceptions of course, but the rest belong to the gloss-over type, the kind of people who never face facts if they are unpleasant, because they can afford not to. I was on leave ten days ago, before my husband embarked for the East. We stayed in an hotel in London. I saw two girls from here with wedding rings and temporary husbands with them, also from here! It is inevitable. It is war.'

As we reach my hotel the conversation ceases. Madge's friends arrive. We repair to a private sitting-room, and pass the time away in singing, dancing, and drinking until ten minutes to ten, when I insist on their leaving so as not to be late.

Madge stays behind. 'Aren't you coming, Madge?' a red-haired A.S.C. driver asks. 'No,' she replies. 'I'm going to stay on and talk to the general. I have a pass until midnight.' 'Oh, oh, oh,' they all cry out, 'and very nice too!' 'Say what you like,' says Madge, 'you'll think it anyhow; one more scandal in Boulogne won't matter!' 'And a general too,' chimes in redhead.

Madge and I talk on until eleven-thirty, when she gets up to go.

I say good night, and see her into her car. She waves a cheery *au revoir* and disappears into the darkness. 'Good thing if they were all like her,' I muse, 'and what a topper her husband is – wish I could have got him for command of one of my battalions; but then, he almost surely would have been killed – he has a better chance in Mespot.'

I turn in, but my luck is out as there is an air-raid in Boulogne. The noise of the Archies keeps me awake, between these white sheets, as no guns ever do in the line, when I am between blankets. 'It's out of place, I suppose,' I say next morning at breakfast, to a man at a table near me, 'to have bombs and sheets, luxury and inferno all on at the same time.' 'You know they dropped a big bomb into base headquarters?' he asks. 'No, I didn't,' I reply. 'They killed many clerks and what-nots, but what they are most concerned over, of course, is the papers and records.' 'I'm not surprised,' I remark; 'the base always does put more store in paper than bullets! And regards men as machines!' Arriving 'home' – for I have become accustomed to regard the Welch brigade as home – I am delighted to find the Ulster Division is on our left. My old brigadier gives a dinner party for me at Metz, and invites those of the old gang who survive to meet me. We have oysters from Amiens. Alas! the toll of war has led to the amalgamation of the old 9th with another battalion, so that it has lost its individuality, although it fought as the 9th – Ormerod's old 9th – at Messines and Paschendale: in the former doing well, in the latter never having a chance, as it was slaughtered in its trenches before it got going. One-eyed

Haslett had come back as second-in-command, only to receive another fierce wound which put him out of the war for good, in so far as France is concerned. Woods, now a D.S.O. colonel, moves to England and thence to Russia, where he picks up a C.M.G. Montey commands the 15th Rifles. Hine has gone back to his own regiment. Only old Jim Newton remains to father the amalgamated flock and he doesn't like it. Nine months of war has completely altered my old unit – some few have become exalted, while still more have left their bones in Belgium. At dinner I hear sad news. Faith, a staff officer whom I knew, who had a wonderfully good-looking wife, fell on misfortune. The girl, to whom he was devoted, had taken to drugs, drink and adultery, during his absence at the war. He seldom went home on leave; he who funked nought else, funked that. Applying for a regimental appointment, he assumed command of a battalion in Flanders, and saw his chance. 'Why should I live in misery?' he evidently thought to himself. Walking out in daylight into an ill-defined no man's land, he asked for it, and got it. Death. His body could not be reached. Where was the good? After all 'dead bodies are no damned use in war' is as true today as when the remark was first made. The fall of Faith in Flanders rang only half the curtain down on one of the saddest of war tragedies. The final act was still to come.

It is as well to say now that in 1917 a serious menace appeared. By that time the British Army was the British nation in khaki. Youngsters who, in the normal way, would have gone to university, trade, business or profession, had joined the service, and over them the Army command was placed *in loco parentis*. It was unequal to the task, not because it wanted to avoid responsibility, but because it knew no better.

In 1917, I urged with all my might that spirits should not be allowed to be drunk in the army in France. These were forbidden in France to the French. With us, far from being forbidden, the drinking of spirits was made easy. Canteens and clubs behind the lines and at the bases were stocked with alcohol.

Profiteers made money out of it at the expense of the youth of the nation, which, had there been no war, would never have learnt the taste of strong drink, at least until years of discretion had been reached.

As it turned out, families and homes were broken up through this evil, habits being introduced into homes which, but for the war and the drink evil, would have remained unshackled and free.

The legacy we have with us now. I know of at least a dozen cases myself, where the habits of drink and the vices associated with it and the loss of control due to it, have reacted on men who today are only in their early thirties.

It was a lamentable failure on the part of responsible soldiers to realise their position. It had to do with profit and selfishness. To expel whisky, the one whisky and soda a day men in high places would have had to give it up altogether. But why not? Men were giving up their lives!

In 1917 a class of men were being granted commissions, who until then had had no idea of rising to the heights of social beverages – whisky, gin, cocktails and the like. The acquisition of a star does not itself alter a man's desires, if he is given a chance and is allowed to do as he would wish.

Half the cases of indiscipline on the part of officers which came through my hands (and there were a good many) were, directly or indirectly, attributable to drinking being made easy. And in addition, of course, the physique suffered.

I have heard it said that the British Empire was consolidated with the aid of 'baccy, beer and the Bible, plus the gallant efforts of the British soldier. I have no doubt about the latter; but the record of beer and the Bible in the war leaves me stone cold. Both sides suffered from alcoholic debauchery, while both used the Bible as propaganda for hate!

General Nugent, up to the mark as ever, knowing we know his front and the habits of the enemy, honours us by seeking information for raids and reconnaissance. The spirit of George Gaffikin returns to his own Orangemen to aid them in their task!

The time has now nearly arrived for us to make our own bow to the Gouzeaucourt sector, at least for the time being. We have been in the wilderness for over nine months and in action practically the whole time. There is rumour of a fresh push in our area. Did not General Byng, the army commander, go up to the O. Pip in Gonnelieu? Are not pigeon lofts being brought into the area? If the big pots wish to disguise their intentions from us they should manage their business better! 'We are going out to refit and train for the push,' says discerning Plunkett, seldom wrong. 'I know it, because one of our fellows heard Dados say he wouldn't issue more clothing.'

Before we leave we are to be woken up to the fact that the Germans are still active. Our right brigade is in for it. One of its officers quietly saunters over to the enemy lines one day, with maps. He was seen to do it by a sentry who thought, quite naturally, he was reconnoitring in a foolish manner, as he was exposing himself. Shortly after, in broad daylight, the Boche comes over after breakfast, almost reaching the brigade headquarters on our right, pulling old miners from their work on tunnels, cooks from their cooking, together with many other dumbfounded people from their trenches, back with them across no man's land, hardly sustaining a casualty in their effort! They had worked by the map – *our map!* 'Wish to goodness they would try and do it to me!' says old Andrews as he puts out a defensive flank on his own initiative. 'We'd larn 'em!'

It was decided by the gods that be that this mis-used Brigade on our right should have its revenge. Every conceivable kind of device is collected with which to give Fritz what for. Flame throwers, bombs full of incendiary matter and flying flames to light the sky for the assaulting troops at night. Lights, stars, shells, rockets and blue, red, green and orange drops give colour to the scheme. Zero hour is reasonable. It coincides with our dinner. We decide to give a dinner party in a sunken road near our dugouts, not far from the quarry, in order that our friends may see what Brock can do elsewhere than at the Crystal Palace.

The hour arrives. The guests sit down. The sky is ablaze with magnificent illuminations. The oysters are being consumed. 'I don't believe in all this publicity for dirty work,' says old Andrews, 'I believe in the dark' . . . *Bang!* . . . behind us, not fifty yards away, drops a shell, a premature from one of our own guns! Some jump in their seats, others disappear under the table! All is again quiet, confidence is restored. Afterwards we sit on the bank and smoke cigars. 'Brock has done us very well,' says Kennedy, 'but where the devil does the war come in?' 'It doesn't,' I reply.

At last the orders for relief arrive. I am due for leave. I decide to go home a week before the relief and to get back just when the men are settled down at Gouay, as then I shall be required for the training.

A pal in the Ulster Division is going home shortly, on leave. We arrange for him to be at Fins at 7 a.m. next day so that I can drive him to Boulogne. I reach Fins at the appointed time. There is no sign of my friend. I wait half an hour; I can't wait much longer, as if I do I shall miss the boat. I ring up. 'Has Ogden left?' I ask. 'He was killed by a stray at dawn,' is the reply. 'Thank you,' I say, and put down the receiver. I push off. We pass two subalterns on the road, obviously lorry jumping. 'Do you want a lift? Jump in. Where do you want to get to?' I ask. 'Amiens, Sir,' is the reply. 'Don't pass it,' I answer. 'How would Boulogne do, you could lorry back?' They hesitate. 'I'm coming back to-night, Sir,' says the driver. 'I have to get a repair done to the car, I could bring the officers back.' 'Splendid, Sir,' says the spokesman of the two.

I am in command of the leave boat on the way over, so have a free cabin to myself on deck. The sea is dead calm. 'Who is that girl?' I say aloud; the

ship's adjutant looks up. 'Which, Sir?' he asks.
'Oh, nothing,' I say, 'I thought I saw a friend of
mine, that's all.' I look again, the girl turns back.
She is in uniform. Yes, it is Madge. I leave the deck
cabin and interrupt her. 'What are you doing here?'
I ask. She had not seen me. Her face lights up, but
she is calm. 'You haven't heard?' she says. 'Heard
what?' I answer with a pang – for I realise the truth.
'He was killed ten days ago, thank God outright, in
the van.' A tiny tear forces its way through, which
she brushes aside. 'This war is hell, Frank,' she
says, 'give me some tea in the train will you? I'll
pay the difference in fare – a driver goes third!
perhaps they'll court-martial you for eating with a
female other rank?' 'I'll get another Pullman ticket
on board,' I say, 'I go off the ship first as C.O.;
You can carry this haversack and follow me.' 'Poor
Madge!' I think, 'how she loved him! how plucky
she is! British women are the best in the world. It
is a pity they can't order their lives so as to abolish
their own sufferings, as it is they who suffer most in
war. Why can't we do without it?'

We pass through the garden county of Kent, and
as I look out of the window I say to Madge: 'There
are times when I think no war is worth the candle;
yet, when I look on these green fields and fruit trees
and gaze down the valley at Dunton Green towards
Westerham, and then look over at you, immediately

opposite me, and see your pink cheeks, pretty features and definitely positive countenance, I feel, anyhow, we must fight to the last man to protect these beautiful things!'

'Yes,' she replies, thoughtfully, 'that's all right; you must fight now to the last man, because you're in it – we're all in it – but, when the war is over, you and I and all of us must again fight to see that war is abolished, and that we settle our disputes as Christians and Jews and Hindoos, and all the rest of them should, I mean by peaceful means. This I owe to Harry and to Harry's –' she dropped her eyes and blushed. 'I'm so glad Madge, I didn't know,' I reply.

As we approach Chislehurst I say to Madge: 'I may be in trouble at Victoria. A man named Ogden was to have come down with me to Boulogne to go on leave. He was killed early this morning. His wife, a mere child, whom I know very slightly, was to have met him. I don't know if she knows. If she doesn't and is at the station, I shall have to break the news – otherwise she will be in even a worse stew – I hope she isn't there.' 'I must help you, Frank,' she says. 'How like you, in all your own trouble,' I answer.

At Victoria we do not hurry off the train. The usual crowd is at the gate, mostly women; but I see a proud father or two looking anxiously through the rails.

At last we walk down the platform to the barrier. 'There's Mrs. Ogden and her little girl,' I say, 'now we're for it!'

The girl does not recognise me, and I could quite easily have escaped. I approach her and salute. 'Mrs. Ogden?' I enquire. 'You are General Crozier?' she says sweetly. 'I did not recognise you in your general's uniform!' And then the inevitable question is put. 'Have you seen my husband? He was to have crossed today. Perhaps he's on another boat,' she asks. 'I have not seen Odgen today,' I say, 'he is not on another boat, he's——' I hesitate. 'Tell me the worst,' she pleads, clutching my arm. 'Is it hospital or——?' she asks. 'Or,' I answer, beckoning Madge to grip her other arm. She swings and sways. I ask a G.R. man to lend a hand. He brings a first aid restorative and we lead her to a waiting room. 'I don't know her address,' I whisper to Madge. 'Mrs. Ogden,' she says quietly, 'my husband and yours have both joined up together on the other side of the barrage. I see them both. They are getting on splendidly. They beg us do the same – "Courage!" I hear them gaily shouting in their old way. "Victory for England! Look after the . . . the . . . kids," I hear them plead. "No surrender. Keep our flags flying high."'

The charm has worked. 'Leave her to me, Frank,' says Madge. 'Where are you staying?

Telephone me tonight at eight to my mother's flat, and I'll let you know how she is. Go now, this G.R. angel will see to us, won't you?' she asks, smiling in her sweet way at the stalwart veteran who really feels his war job for England is at last at hand.

I dine at Pobos, a fashionable night club, with a friend, a legal man, whose son is with us, and ring up Madge at eight. 'All is well,' she tells me. The two war widows, the one with a child, the other expecting one, are to be great friends, united by a common bond which unites as no other can. 'Go and enjoy yourself,' she adds, 'you need it. God grants strength on these occasions! Night, night!' She rings off. 'Wonderful woman,' I muse. We sit on talking until two a.m. I drink strong coffee while my friend keeps a bottle of brandy busy after champagne. 'I thought,' I say, 'these places had to shut early, and not sell liquor after ten?' 'You thought wrong, old man, you come from the backwoods, "the mug line" the fellows in there call it,' he says, pointing to a private room. 'There are probably ten men in there now, at least, who are making huge fortunes out of your war; pretend to go in by mistake and look at them; and in there,' he says, pointing to another door, 'I will also show you something else which will interest you.' I open the door and behold a dozen or so fat profiteers 'doing themselves well.' 'They seem to be having a very good war!'

I remark, as I return to my host. 'Now,' he says, 'just follow me, stand behind me and look and listen.' My friend enters a small room on the right, 'Good evening, gentlemen,' he says in his nicest manner. They look up. On the table is champagne and brandy. 'Good *morning*,' says one of the two adapters – for they are politicians – sitting in easy chairs at their ease. 'Let me see, Mr. Rankes, is it?' he adds enquiringly. 'No, that is not my name,' replies my host; 'Good morning' – We withdraw to our original position, as the official war bulletin sometimes says.

'Yes,' I say, 'I recognise them from their pictures in the paper.' 'Well then,' he says, 'you will now know why *some* people can get a drink here when they like! In one room you have the profiteers and financiers, in another the cabinet ministers!' 'But where do you come in?' I ask. 'Oh, I'm only the bloke who can put 'em all in jail if I like,' he says with a laugh, 'they have to suffer me!'

I spend two weeks on leave, during which period I see *The Bing Boys* five times, and come to the conclusion that George Robey and Violet Loraine are together one of our greatest war assets. And from them, strengthened by them, I hasten to join the other Byng Boys on a bigger stage, in the area of Cambrai.

Some weeks after my return to France I receive

a letter from Madge telling me about Mrs. Ogden, whom she has been looking after ever since the terrible tragedy was enacted at Victoria station when she first learnt of her husband's death. Madge is always very far-seeing and thoughtful. She combines charm of manner and artistic taste with sound common sense.

I read her letter slowly, while lying out in the long grass in no man's land between the opposing lines, where I have been to 'look round.' The following passage strikes me particularly and I cut it out: – 'Mrs. Ogden is in a dreadful state, poor soul – she says she will never be herself again, which is a bad beginning; but it is wonderful how the Almighty seems to come to the rescue of us poor women in our agony and gives us strength to save ourselves (or should it be souls?) This whole war tragedy is one great "S.O.S." When you send up the "S.O.S." in battle you merely and really mean "Save our lives or life." I hope the war is going to prove to be the *real "S.O.S." of civilisation*. We shall *all* have to work together for this end when we throw off the mask.'

# CHAPTER VII

## THE WELCH EPIC

I HURRY back to the brigade. There is no dawdling now at Boulogne. Is there not training to be done? Has not the Irish girl from the south, whose husband is in Egypt, and whose lover is in the Ulster Division, written to say there is to be a mighty attack at Cambrai next month? She should know! Many military secrets slip out between the sheets, in war!

Despite all else said to the contrary our possible objectives are very long and quite indefinite. We may have to take Bourlon Wood we are told, or throw out outposts twenty miles to the east of it. Much will depend on the break through, most on the tanks and cavalry. As a brigade we are trained to the minute. We have excelled in ceremonial, we shall excel in the harder stuff which draws its inspiration from close order drill. The men are rested. They have worked, drilled, manœuvred, boxed, run, marched and fed as only those can do whose hearts are elsewhere than on their sleeves.

At wood fighting they have 'gone through it' like

176

BOURLON WOOD FROM GRAINCOURT, NOVEMBER, 1917

a knife through butter – damning the consequences, and not counting the loss. Positive thought, positive movement, positive action in all things, is the only thing now to make peace possible. We are positive.

At 6.20 a.m., on November 20th, the tanks go over. The Irish lady was right! We reach Danger Corner in a deluge on 22nd. On that day, a corps commander, through whose formation we pass, confides in me his innermost thoughts in response to my question 'what of the chances?' 'We have done wonderfully,' he says, 'the successes of the first two days have far exceeded our most liberal expectations. All now depends on you and the cavalry; you are to attack Bourlon Wood tomorrow; can you take it? And, if so, can the cavalry break through? Those are the answers to your question,' he adds. 'We'll take the wood on our heads,' I say. 'I'm glad to hear it,' answers the lieutenant-general; 'but I fear the cavalry have lost their thrusters, they have gone to the Tanks, the Flying Corps and the Infantry.' Having rested the horses and ourselves, I decide on a mounted dash to Graincourt, through the mud, in order that we may see the wood in daylight, as we do not know the time of the attack.

We are quite a cavalcade, colonels, majors, company commanders, machine-gun officers, the staff, grooms and gunners make up in all a troop of sixty-odd. Away we dash through the Ulster supports. We pass through what is left of my old battalion. Jameson, a captain, I see. There is no time to stop: moreover, am I not followed by sixty horse? We exchange salutations. On the morrow he dies. Benzie meanwhile has become unhorsed. We push on. Each to his task, we return separately. Late in the night we plod back in the mud to relieve some Yorkshire men. The Tank colonel arrives. All is ready. The hour of advance is settled for 10.30 a.m., on the morrow. The Welch Bantams are faced with their acid test. Will they be found wanting? G.H.Q. evidently does not know its own strength, or has it confused our Welshmen with others? While Andrews is wanting to bet fifty to one against Bourlon village being taken, and a thousand to one on the wood being captured, a G.H.Q. staff officer wants to bet twenty to one against the capture of the wood! 'I wish I'd met the ass,' says Andrews, a few hours later, while lying seriously wounded on a stretcher, outside my dugout; 'he wouldn't have had a bean left with which to go on leave next time!' Of course Andrews is intuitively right. He knows all the men. Benzie wants to take the village, in addition to his own task which he successfully accomplishes in the morning, on the afternoon of the 23rd and then hand it over to others, for safe custody!

Our headquarters at Graincourt are in some

catacombs underneath a church. German-made electric light is still burning, while two German electricians are found on the premises to carry on the work of maintenance. But the little French interpreter finds more. He finds enough explosive matter to blow us all into the next world, ready fused and timed! The Germans, quite unaware of what they sit upon, work on at the electric plant until told to remove the dangerous cargo left behind by their comrades. Seldom have men worked harder!

My final words before the attack are simple. 'Remember Spion Kop,' I say. 'If I want you to come back, come back. I decide your fate. You hold on or die.'

The reader who wishes to follow the fate of the previously discredited and misunderstood little Welshmen can do so in the various histories, though there he will not learn quite all the facts.

In my mind only the salient features, the super-human efforts of brave resolute men, stand out.

Of course the wood is quickly taken; and, what is more important, it is held. The cavalry do not go through. Is the corps commander right? Have they lost their thrusters? There is no 'Spion Kop' where Benzie and Plunkett are concerned; but Kennedy is dead and Andrews is lying on his face, hit through the sciatic nerve. That wound is to keep him out of battle for nine long months until he once more rejoins, limping, to advance to victory. Benzie, being senior, is placed in command in the wood. Benzie supervises the left, Plunkett the right.

Morton, the argumentative estate agent, is badly hit, while leading his company, and later, lying helpless on the ground, a tank travels over him and squashes him to death.

Halfway through the battle it became clear that the wood might be lost at any moment owing to both flanks being in the air, if something were not done. I have the wood stocked with rations, water and ammunition, and decide that we shall, if necessary, hold out in a state of siege. This policy was the direct negation of the tactics employed on Spion Kop in 1900; but in any case none of my senior officers would have dreamt of abandoning the wood, for any cause. These tactics if employed on every occasion in the absence of orders are well worth while, because isolated 'islands' of resolute men, able to shoot straight and often, always exact a heavy toll from advancing masses and cause a delay worth even such sacrifice.

The battle is a soldier's one. The ebb and flow is like a balanced contest between two tug-of-war teams. The German counter-attacks are terrific. We hold on. Highlanders arrive to reinforce, Yorkshiremen and dismounted hussars fill the gaps. Still the fight goes on. A few men with flagging energy and less staying power than the rest, lose their heads and some of them their lives, in consequence. They fly from danger only to encompass disaster. A revolver emptied 'into the brown' accounts for five; a Lewis gun fired into the panic-stricken mass puts many on the grass and undergrowth. 'This position must be held' shouts an officer in stentorian tones: 'get back, and if you don't I blow you from the wood with powder.' Calm comes.

Meanwhile an officer, slightly wounded, seeks to pass to safety by virtue of his scratch. He is put back to fight, and is forced with others up the hill again, there to die.

Young Amery-Parkes, a major of twenty-two years of age, in command of machine guns, obeys the spirit of the order. He loses every gun and gun-crew save a few, but leaves a monument – a long, heaped-up pile of dead Germans.

George Franks of 19th Hussars comes into my dugout and upsets a bottle of port and six glasses. We curse him!

The Guards arrive, a strength as usual, even in their very name. They help us hold on and then we depart. Great has been the carnage in our ranks. The little Welshmen are no more, but those who do remain are there to carry on the torch. We struggle out by night in November mud which we have seen before elsewhere.

I see the red lamp of the brigade and struggle to my blankets while faithful Starrett waits me. 'Where are we?' I ask. 'In a vault, Sir,' is the reply. 'Jerry took the coffins out long ago and made it into a telephone exchange for the Hindenburg Line.' 'Flash a light,' I order; he switches on his torch. 'Good gracious,' I say, 'who are they whose feet I see in the coffin nitches – dead men in boots?' 'Your staff, Sir,' laughs Starrett, as well as he can, for he is very tired too. 'They're so done they would sleep anywhere, but I have a fine place for you, Sir; you have a slab of your own to sleep on and a room to yourself. I guess a big man must have been put in there some time. 'But don't you think the place smells funny, Sir?' he says. 'I have never smelt such a diabolical stench in my life,' I say; 'a cross between dead bodies and old wood.' 'That's the coffins,' says Starrett. 'Well,' I remark, 'I don't know how these officers can sleep here, in this fug and musty smell.' 'They'd sleep anywhere, they're nearly dead themselves, and there's no other place; you lie down now as you are, here's some tea coming, and go to sleep,' he says. When Starrett thought he had to exercise his authority over me, and knew full well I was too far gone to notice, he always left out his 'Sirs,'– and it always acted! But he generally had a cup of tea to balance matters up! I cannot sleep. I fight Germans in my semi-conscious state, and find myself grovelling

December 20th., 1917.

Dear Sir,

I am very much obliged to you for your letter and for your courtesy in sending me a report of the doings of your Brigade in the recent fighting. I am most interested, as you knew I would be, in this narrative, and I would like to compliment you on the gallant way in which your brave men seem to have carried out what was a very difficult piece of work, and I appreciate too very much your words of praise about my own countrymen. I knew they would fight well, and they have upheld in an honourable way the traditions of their forefathers. But if they have proved themselves in this fight, it must be to a large extent due to their leadership, and it is a compliment to yourself that you are able to give such a splendid account of your men. Please accept my best congratulations.

Wishing you & the fine
men you command and a new Year of Victory.

Yours faithfully,

D. Lloyd George

Brig. Gen. F.P.Crozier, D.S.O.

A LETTER RECEIVED FROM THE PRIME MINISTER ON THE OCCASION OF THE CAPTURE OF BOURLON WOOD BY THE WELCH BANTAMS, DECEMBER, 1917

on the coffinless floor. In the morning we march on.

Near by, at Havraincourt, we pass the chief – Sir Douglas – erect on his charger, wearing tin hat and gas respirator at the alert. 'A chiefly figure,' I remark. 'A chief,' is the reply.

The chief asks the men who they are. They tell him. 'Well done,' I hear him say over and over again. 'Well done.'

We arrive at a cold and comfortless camp, but thanks to the kindness of a Young Men's Christian Association official we are given extra warmth, and hot beverages. The night is perishingly cold.

Our French interpreter arrives back to the fold. 'Do you know where you spent last night, General?' he asks. 'In a tomb,' I reply. 'Yes,' he says, 'in the family vault of the great Havraincourt family, where their ancestors lay for years until the château became the front line and the Boche wanted cover from fire, and lead from the coffins!' 'How awful,' I say, 'what a thought!' 'More than a thought – a reality,' replies the little man, 'and by God,' he adds, 'these swine will pay for their sacrilege some day.' 'Oh, I think you're wrong there,' I say. 'I quite see they had to make the line where it was and we have yet to prove they broke open the coffins: we say they did, of course, and naturally they used good concrete cover. I don't see why you should draw the line anywhere in war. After all, we used the vault as cover from weather!' 'Yes,' says the little Frenchman, 'you did, I didn't; and you cooked your eggs and bacon there too, and then ate them in it. Fancy turning a family vault into your kitchen and bedroom combined!' 'Well,' I say, 'I don't think we did much harm; and in any case we lost three thousand of our best Welshmen out of four for your French people, so you can't grumble! Where did *you* sleep?' I ask. 'In a tent at the French Mission,' he answered. 'A British tent?' I ask laughingly. 'Anyhow I think we owe you a debt, you saved us from being blown up in a church,' I say; 'and you and I used the church premises for killing Germans! Sacrilege, what?' 'Call them Huns, General,' he says.

After big battle the reckoning comes! Nine months' toil is wiped out in three days! The wounded suffer greatly. Four hundred German prisoners have been employed in carrying British wounded in the shell-swept area, in which many Germans are killed while carrying out this duty. Why not? They had been kept at their mission of relief of suffering for three whole days. The work of evacuation was difficult owing to the bad roads and congestion. Shells take precedence of useless wounded men. At one time hundreds of dying and wounded lay in the open at Graincourt, awaiting their turn for removal to the base, while shells exploded among them, killing many. There was no means of preventing this occurrence. War is savage – and mankind is its victim.

On the evening of the third day after the tumult, we travel in one short train – it took nine to bring us up to the slaughter, and find ourselves on the Bapaume battlefield of the previous year in the midst of brick and rubble.

'Which is the way to le Coupe Guleule?' I ask a road traffic-control policeman, on finding myself at a road junction in open country. 'This *is* le Coupe Guleule, Sir,' he replies, saluting. The fate of war had befallen this village which had been entirely effaced from off the earth.

During dinner a staff officer is called to the 'phone. Returning, he tells me we are to go into the line tomorrow at Bullecourt, south of Arras. 'The Boche counter-attacked,' he says, 'and regained all our captures. They saturated Bourlon Wood with gas and killed thousands there and in the vicinity. They even retook Gouzeaucourt, and from our old quarry a divisional commander escaped in his pyjamas. The Guards, as usual, saved the situation; and the line is now practically as it was before the tanks went over. The Irish Division is to come out to go into the battle, if it is wanted, while we take their place in Tunnel Trench, as we are so weak.'

'Thank goodness, we are going into the line at

once,' I say; 'it is best for all, provided they send us men. I can never sleep for a fortnight after a big battle, the reaction is so great; but a new line with its new problems to solve acts as an antidote.' The brigadier whom I relieve is an old friend. We last met when troopers together in South Africa, on the Tugela seventeen years before.

One of my colonels, Plunkett, was this brigadier's sergeant-major at the beginning of the war. 'Plunkett is rather a marvel,' he says, 'a Distinguished Conduct Medal, a commission, a M.C., and a colonel in three years!' 'Yes,' I reply, 'I am putting him in for a V.C., for Bourlon and I hope he will get a brigade shortly. A Cavalry brigadier motored forty miles to tell me of his wonderful conduct with 15th Hussars in the wood, which of course I knew about; but it was nice of 15th to make a point of sending over their brigadier.'

'He was recommended for the V.C. on the Retreat,' replies my friend, 'and only got the D.C.M. instead. I hope he will be more successful this time.'

The relief is complete.

Plunkett clears up a bit of hostile line opposite his front. We follow the movements of his Bourlon survivors through our glasses. We count twenty-two prisoners being hunted across no man's land to our lines. Only five arrive! 'You must have let

seventeen prisoners escape!' I say to the captain of
a company later. 'We never let prisoners escape,
Sir,' is the answer I receive . . . 'sometimes they
attempt to!' The scar of battle leaves its mark on
Plunkett. He faints in the line while struggling
through the mud. The strain of 'thirty hours' continued and sustained valour' for which he was
recommended for the Cross has upset his heart.
He is invalided home, thereby losing his brigade.
He does not get the V.C., but a D.S.O. Indeed, as
I have already put him in for a half-yearly D.S.O.,
he amasses two. The blue pencil is mightier than
the sword – once the battle is over. It is easier to
hold the line against repeated enemy counter-
attacks than to persuade an officer fifty miles away
at G.H.Q., that 'thirty hours' valour' is better than a
flash in the pan action, however brave the latter
may be.

'But he was only doing his duty!' I am told by a
red-banded clerk-officer, who has never seen a shot
fired. 'Then,' I reply, 'where do you draw the line?
Every act is one of duty! If every man behaved as
does Plunkett, in action, every objective would be
taken, every point would be held, provided the wire
is cut, or all would die! The truth is the war has
made people dishonest. Men are scrambling for
honours and rewards, and people are recommended
for rewards on account of friendship, favouritism,

and the like, on a larger scale than ever in our time before. After each big battle, I have a bigger and bigger fight about the rewards for my men. The lists are chock-a-block with names put in by favour; and when occasionally a hard-fighting man without interest gets recommended, he is left out, as there is no one to push him! It is a scandal and a slur!' 'But, General, look at the thousands of awards made!' says the officer-clerk. 'Quite so,' I say, 'I can tell you offhand of twenty unmerited D.S.O.'s awarded in this war! and,' I add, 'in order to shelve the matter, the line of least resistance is taken. If I put up a hundred names for immediate awards after a big battle, I am told to put a great many of them on the half-yearly list. This has happened now: it will probably happen again before April, when the June list is prepared. I am then given perhaps twenty places in the list, but I have fifty piled up names, put back by Corps, for the list and twenty names of my own, for which the list is meant. It's all wrong. That's why I recommended, when asked, that all honours should be abolished for the duration! There's no good having decorations unless they are given the right way!'

Although the war has made me almost impervious to shocks, a telephone message which I receive after Christmas yet makes me quiver.

I am wanted on the telephone. 'Moore speaking,

General,' I hear, as I take up the receiver. 'I have bad news for you' . . . there is a pause. 'Yes,' I say, 'let's have it quick' . . . 'You are to lose the S.W.B.'s, the R.W.F., and one of the Welch battalions, whichever you like: there are not enough recruits in Wales for the Welch Division and your Welch Brigade. Brigades are being reduced to a three-battalion establishment, so you get the East Surreys from the 120th Brigade, and 21st Middlesex from the 121st.' 'Anything else?' I ask. 'I'll give up 17th: they lost heaviest, and Brown of S.W.B's is now colonel of 18th Welch. I presume the other two brigades do not retain their *worst* battalions!' Moore sympathises with me, and the curtain rings down on the Welch Brigade, which fought its way to glory while it carried a whole division on its shoulders.

I am tired. We are at Mercatel, a desolate spot near Arras. I sneak ten days' leave while the new units are assembling and being made up. We know we are in for a rough time in March. For the first time during the war I feel this leave will be my last. I put in a theatre a night and a matinée when possible. I say nothing about my forebodings to my wife, but she knows intuitively, as does even the child aged seven. The time comes for parting. They come to the station to see me off by the staff train from platform three at Charing Cross. I give the child a pound note to buy a book or two, and to keep her quiet. We are just on time. There is no hanging about on the platform. A fond farewell, a last embrace. The guard blows his whistle. We are off. They stand waving until I'm out of sight, far over the ugly iron bridge spanning Old Father Thames. I vow to myself I shall never come on leave again, even if I get through. Two days later I receive a letter in France: 'After you left,' I read, 'we went to the hotel and cried ourselves to sleep, Baba in my arms.' 'My God, this is a hell of a war,' I say to my orderly officer, as I get ready to inspect the two newly arrived battalions. 'What's wrong, Sir?' asks the lad. 'Oh, nothing,' I say. Starrett looks at me; 'you didn't take your medicine this morning, Sir,' he says. 'I have a letter from Mrs. Crozier here about you, saying I'm to take care of you, but how can I do that if you won't do as I tell you?' The orderly officer looks horrified! He is new to us! He doesn't understand! Starrett and I burst out laughing. It's the only way. Humour pulls us through the war.

# CHAPTER VIII

## THE STONE WALL

WHEN the hammer blow fell in 1918, the Germans were casting the dice for their final fling.

We are ready with one old war-scarred battalion and two new ones – the Middlesex and Surreys. True, the latter had both been associated with the attack on Bourlon village; but as the venture had not been a success, they still lack confidence. To the Middlesex comes a new commander, one Metcalfe, an old soldier of some fifty-odd summers, a county chief constable, sportsman, and musketry expert. He has not been in France before. His experience of war is *nil*. 'His battalion needs much training,' I say to my brigade major. 'I fear he has not enough experience of modern battle to change them in the time available – and they are not much good now.' I am mistaken. From March 21st to 25th Metcalfe is a stone wall when necessary, a thrusting lance when required. The truth is that in resisting the German onslaught, apart from physical fitness, the only qualities necessary for the upholding

of the British name in March are those possessed
by the English gentleman of the pre-industrial
regime, of whom Metcalfe is one. He held the line
for England with his Diehards, because of what
was in him – blood and breeding. Bombs, bullets,
flame, gas and shells of all sorts and kinds, can
kill or rip up thousands, cold steel 'with a twist
in it' makes a nasty gash; but these things, with the
addition of privation and exhaustion, do not deter
or frighten the English gentleman of the ancient
line from doing his duty or dying in the attempt.
So Metcalfe drawing strength and inspiration from
the past, plays the game, turning himself into a
two-year-old one minute, a veteran tactician at
another – and wins! Not far from him, Benzie,
now with Highland troops of another formation
also makes history for Scotland – but alas – severely
wounded, he falls, to be *hors de combat* for the
remainder of the war, thus losing his brigade-pro-
motion. Brown of the Welch, a product of Pope and
Benzie, acts up to the traditions of his corps. We
draw back by degrees – but only as a ruse. On the
night of the 23rd, the struggle is intense. Hand
to hand fighting brings sons of Germany literally
into the Welch grip. They have them by the throat
in deathly vice-like hold. I send up a subaltern,
G. V. Jones, with thirty men, the only reserve left,
to Ervillers in a lorry, to stem the tide, 'Fire,' he

THE RUINS OF ERVILLERS FROM WHICH LIEUT. G. V. JONES, 18TH WELCH REGT.
EJECTED A GERMAN REGIMENT, MARCH, 1918

commands; a fusillade flashes out. They are bluffed. They think a new regiment has arrived. Thirty Welshmen put a German regiment to flight! Mory shall be recaptured too, I think. Later I ring up an officer: 'Now is your chance,' I say, 'nip into Mory, no one is there to speak of, their reserves are late – do it now.' 'What's that I hear?' I say. 'Can't!' 'Don't understand the meaning of the word,' I say. 'Lead your men to the objective,' I order, 'or, if you *can't*, come back here. I'll send up Jones to do it for you, and you can be tried by court martial.' He thinks twice and attacks, gaining much kudos thereby!

We are allied with the brigade of Guards of 31st Division on our left, so our flank is safe; and as I talk with their brigadier a staff officer approaches me. 'What are we to do with all the liquor in the Expeditionary Force Canteen?' he asks, 'there are dozens of full cases and bottles on the shelves.' 'Ask corps to get away what they can in the next three hours, we can't guarantee to hold the place longer, and destroy what is left,' I say. 'Don't let the men near the bottles on any account alone – a field officer must supervise the destruction.' 'What about the cigars?' he asks. 'Oh anyone can have them,' I reply. 'No man has ever yet, that I know of, been put in the guardroom for over-smoking!' That afternoon hundreds of bottles of brandy, champagne, whisky, liquors, port and gin are broken. The gutters of Ervillers flow with alcohol! Better that than have it nourish sick Germans back to life in order that they may come to destroy us again; better still than flowing down the parched throats of British soldiers in action, and thus rendering them unfit to take their places in the stone wall!

Next morning as I walk round the firing line I see a funny sight. Masses of German infantry, in close order, are approaching, six hundred yards away, while men from Middlesex and Wales pump lead into the human mass, killing by the score. Never was target like it, perhaps! And the marksmanship is good, the rapid fire excellent. 'Even the third-class shots are in their element,' says a subaltern to me. The machine guns mow down thousands. And in each British mouth is a big cigar held at an angle, in the teeth, while in order to effect a balance, as it were, on the heads – at an opposite angle, rest the tin hats. 'Bairnsfather at his best,' I say. We lost a great deal of kit from shell fire – and Starrett is upset. 'Your best coat is gone, Sir,' he says. The men begin to show signs of stress. 'Will relief never come?' we ask ourselves inwardly, but not aloud. 'Hang on, hang on,' I urge, 'at all costs!'

The corps commander rings up direct. 'How are you getting on,' he asks. 'We're on the move,' I tell him. 'Good heavens, don't say so,' he says, 'not an inch further back can we afford!' 'It's all right, Sir,' I reassure him, 'when we move without orders it's only towards the enemy, not away from him! We've got Mory again.' He is astonished.

We are to be relieved at dusk. Alas! on the way to us the relievers are deflected to check a sudden enemy rush from the south. More delay.

At this juncture I am faced with that test which comes at least once, it seems, in the life of every man – the putting into effect the practice of one's principles – summed up proverbially in the words: 'Practise what you preach.'

For nearly four years I have drummed the lesson of the abandonment of Spion Kop into all and sundry alike. Now I am faced myself with a similar situation. Our position had become precarious. The right flank had been driven in more than once in the last few hours. On the left were our saviours – the Guards. We, in the centre, looked like being attacked in rear from the south.

Rumour has it that German patrols are in the neighbourhood of Gommie-court, where I have my headquarters in deep catacombs.

In the catacombs there is utter chaos. In addition to my own there are the headquarters of other infantry brigades, artillery groups, signallers and the like. Seldom, surely, was there ever such congestion. In the midst of all this Harry Graham, the divisional commander's A.D.C. arrives. 'Clear all these oddments away,' I tell him!

The brilliant librettist of 'The Maid of the Mountains' looks at me in blank astonishment! Easier would it be for mountains to be moved! But I see great danger. If it is true, I think, as it quite well might be, that enemy patrols are at our door, then three German private soldiers could capture the entire staffs and signallers, in the catacombs, for there is only one narrow entrance and no other means of exit, and the steps are steep. I move my headquarters to some old huts and advise others of their danger, and, in doing so, cross the open under observed shell fire. The enemy is very close. At the moment of arrival at our new headquarters, which, although exposed to view perhaps and undoubtedly vulnerable from the air, were not a death trap, I received intelligence that the brigade on our right had retired and that the guards on our left were also coming back. We had received no orders to move. It is now dark. We wait. I feel sure there must have been orders issued for our withdrawal as the guards are moving back, and they never move back without orders.

I ask them. 'Yes, we received orders an hour ago,' says their brigade major. I send my own groom with a personal letter asking for instructions and point out the danger.

'If morning comes,' I write, 'and we are seen, as we shall be, out in the blue, as we are now, we shall be wiped out.'

My duty is clear. The lesson of Spion Kop is at my own feet! The words I burnt into the souls of my subalterns apply equally to me. 'Never give any excuse for retiring, don't retire unless you're ordered to,' I told them in 1914.

Someone had blundered, but we mustn't.

At last the moment arrives. We may go! We have lost masses of manhood – but the line is intact. The spirit of Wales and London is inviolable. Metcalfe, the Stonewall, goes trout fishing, while the King of England walks quietly among his sleeping soldiers.

# CHAPTER IX

## THE PRICE OF POLITICS

By 1918 the question of memory became a serious consideration in my make up. During big battles I invariably lost my power for remembering names, owing to want of sleep, on about the third day; so I always had the names of my colonels and senior officers tabulated in my notebook for reference. All other things I could remember. I did all other things and met situations as they arrived, almost automatically; but names even of men I knew quite intimately escaped me.

I also used to make the most stupid spelling mistakes in writing reports at all times in 1918, a fact possibly due to a lack of newspaper and book reading; so I invariably carried a Collins' Gem Dictionary in my pocket to meet this lapse.

My young staff captain entirely lost the use of his legs for two days, at the end of the March battle, owing to fatigue. I have heard of brigade and divisional commanders who used to read yellow-backed novels during the process of big battles; but

I also used to hear of many battles being lost! Far too many commanders treated the war period as one of 'normality,' which showed a lack of appreciation of the situation. War is never 'normal,' but the great war was entirely different from any other that ever had been. The Big Bugs thought in terms of millions, both of men and money, and left it at that. Our duty was to conserve man-power. That took me all my time, both in battle and in the 'normal' war periods of training and attrition, for the primary duty of every soldier must always be to conserve his life for his country when he can, which entails a minute knowledge of technique; but to be able to sell it as dearly as he can for his country if and when the necessity arrives.

There was no good in combing England for man-power if we read novels and write reports instead of doing things.

Bleeding, bruised, dirty, tired, with hearts intact and faith unshaken we reach rest. As the men lie in slumber deep the King of England again walks round to look at his subject soldiers temporarily done, only to revive once more at the trumpet blast.

The interpreter and some of the staff take a joy ride to a big town to fetch me razor and blades, soap and handkerchiefs, a pair of brushes, and some pyjamas, and other necessary articles of equipment, to replace the articles destroyed by shell fire. 'They will have a good dinner, anyhow,' I say, as I watch them depart; 'not that our cook isn't wonderful; I think he is, seeing his difficulties; but change lends enchantment.' 'Did Reynolds get through?' I ask, the orderly officer shakes his head, 'or Poker?' I add. 'Dead,' replies the boy, 'he tried a good bluff, but the Boches saw him!' 'Poor old Poker,' I say; 'cheery soul if ever there was one.' At this juncture a doctor comes up. 'Morning, Doc,' I say. He salutes and makes suitable reply, 'Colonel Morden should go down or go to a suitable rest house,' he says; 'he's nearly off his head. I've doped him quite a lot, but he wants an entire change.' 'Do what you like with him, Doctor,' I say. 'Last night,' says the Doctor, 'he was found fighting under his bed with a pillow, swearing it was a Boche.' 'Poor devil,' I say, 'he's played out!'

We receive orders to move north by road and lorry.

On the night of 7th – 8th April, we arrive in the line south of Armentières. On the right are the Portuguese. I don't like the feel of things – all is quiet – too quiet. I go down the Portuguese front with a colonel. We walk seven hundred yards and scarcely see a sentry. We examine rifles and ammunition lying about. All are rusty and useless. The bombs are the same. 'Where are the men?' I ask my companion. A snore gives me my answer.

Practically all the front line sleeps heavily and bootless in cubby holes covered with waterproof sheets, while their equipment hangs carelessly about. 'This is a pretty mess,' I say, 'and on our flank. What would old Andrews say?' I add. 'Well, you know what my new men are all like!' says Colonel Brown of the Welch – – – 'Babies!' We walk back to our own line.

'Our communication trenches are fearfully bad,' says the colonel, 'stretchers can't move with ease in them!' 'I know,' I say, 'I'll see what can be done about them, but from what I can see,' I reply, 'I should think we'll be shot up out of this at dawn, *viâ* the rear!' I go back to my headquarters in a farm, and report what I have seen. 'They're always like that,' says a member of the British Mission attached to the Portuguese, on the telephone. 'They shouldn't be there,' I say, 'that's the crime.'

In the early morning of 9th April, a deafening bombardment wakes me up. Before long Starrett arrives. 'Put this on,' he orders, holding out my gas respirator, 'and get dressed at once. You'll be wanted. I'll pack the kit. Get you to the telephone place, it's strong.' I obey!

All is mystery and gas.

The Portuguese bolt and leave the way open to the Germans. Stonewall Metcalfe, 'at rest' in billets, is the first in action in rear of our position.

His second-in-command is killed at his billet door, by a rifle bullet. Our flank is exposed. How I long for that extra battalion taken away in February in order to swell the paper strength of the numbers of the divisions available! It might have saved the Welch today and certainly the Surreys. I am in touch with Brown on the telephone. He is fighting on his front, right and rear. 'You'd better fight back to me,' I order. 'I'll move my headquarters to Bac St. Maur, north of the Lys. Metcalfe has to look after himself.' The Surreys, what of them? I can get no answer to the 'phone call. At last a guttural voice replies: 'Who are you?' he says. I smell a rat. 'This is a Boche on the 'phone,' I say . . . 'It's all up with the Surreys, I'm sure,' I add. I dismiss this battalion from my calculations.

We move back under rifle and machine-gun fire, to the Lys, where we just arrive in time. Our cooks, trench mortar men, orderlies, and oddments form a covering screen. The bridge at Bac St. Maur is barraged by shell fire and impassable, owing to the dead horses of gun teams as well as wrecked guns, waggons and limbers, piled up on it and at its approach. Most of the guns are lost.

A brigadier comes up to reconnoitre with his brigade major. The former is killed, the latter wounded. We get our military equipment away in waggons, but our kit is sacrificed. Starrett, the faithful one, carries my valise for three miles on his back to safety.

We search for a crossing. Time is of most vital importance. We cannot swim across as the canalised banks are too steep; besides our equipment would bear us down. We find the last temporary footbridge intact and walk over.

May, the young staff captain, has opened up a new headquarters, where the signallers are installed. Amery-Parkes is present with a machine gun. We decide to defend the bridge. Amery-Parkes mows them down with his gun. Campbell, the signalling officer, is badly hit. Hone, the brigade major, dashes out and drags him into cover. We find a derelict motor and willing driver. Suddenly the Germans make a desperate effort to take the bridgehead. Amery-Parkes charges. They fail. Parkes is hit in the head and falls. He is dragged into cover.

'Put Amery-Parkes and Campbell in the car,' I order, 'and take them to Croix du Bac. Bring up some S.A.A. and ask the general the situation and tell him ours.'

Amery-Parkes and I have something in common, in that we were both at Wellington. As I help to put him in the car he says to me in a feeble whisper, '*Semper domus floreat*.' He died a few weeks later, but lived to receive a bar to the Military Cross he had gained at Bourlon.

Brown joins me with fifty-eight men, the remains of a battalion.

Stonewall Metcalfe crossed further south with under a hundred men all told. A fresh brigade of another division comes to our rescue. We receive orders to concentrate at Petit Mortier. Meanwhile, Brown and three others, who have had no breakfast (no one else had I am sure) ask leave to go in the car to Steenwerck for a meal, *en passant*. Later we place a Lewis gun in the car and use it in retirement, until 12th April.

We fight on until the 12th, while Metcalfe gains six hundred yards of ground in a counter-attack with the 2nd Royal Scots Fusiliers. The old warrior, badly hit in the leg, at last makes his bow to the firing line for ever. He is perhaps a record. Three months in action, two D.S.O.'s and a bad wound at over fifty years of age. It has been a ghastly let down, but a triumph for certain individuals. If the Portuguese had never entered the line it would not have been so. Aided by fog and a hurricane bombardment, the Germans knew where to attack! The uniforms of the Germans and Portuguese are not dissimilar. Hundreds of Portuguese were mown down by our machine guns, and rifle fire. After all, 'fire at all field grey advancing towards us' was a legitimate order! In discussing this *débâcle* I say, in answer to a question, shortly after our mishap: 'And the fault? Undoubtedly with the military higher command, for permitting the Channel Ports and England, to say nothing of the valuable lives of British soldiers, to be risked. Political considerations may necessitate certain lines of action which may be distasteful to the soldier; but the safety of the line is far above political considerations or expediency; and if first principles are threatened by the politician, the safety of the country thereby being endangered, all that is left for the chief soldier is resignation. Of course, if it is maintained that G.H.Q. did not know the Portuguese divisions were so inferior, there is nothing more to be said – but in that case, neither they nor their mission could have known the difference between a bad soldier and a good one.'

As I make this rather indignant exposition before a somewhat critical audience, at dinner, in Paris, a silence falls over all, until a simple-looking fellow previously unknown to me says: 'Well, what about the Dardanelles? Do you blame Winston for that? He is a politician.' 'I don't blame anybody for the Dardanelles,' I say, 'simply because I wasn't there and know nothing about it. I have had my work cut out to keep my own tiny command efficient. But if Winston had suggested that a part of our line at Gallipoli should be held by monkeys armed with bladders on sticks . . . which I don't suppose he would ever be so foolish as to suggest . . . he is a first-class soldier . . . I should blame him!' 'You're very unkind to the Portuguese, General;' says my host. 'I don't think I am at all,' I say; 'I think G.H.Q. was unkind to them for ever putting them in such a position: they must have known all about them. They caused them to be slaughtered, and they lost us many lives.' 'All of you appear to forget,' says the only other soldier present, 'that the Duke of Wellington used the Portuguese when led by British officers.'

As a brigade we are diminished by degrees. The command of the Middlesex devolves on a subaltern of twenty-one who becomes an acting lieutenant colonel. I take the new C.O. to meet his old C.O. in hospital. There we see the old warrior with leg tied up to the roof, while on the foot flies a miniature Union Jack!

We stay at the Folkestone – into the hall of which there emerges from the bar a red-nosed major of ruddy countenance with green-banded cap. He is obviously half-seas-over. Looking at the baby-faced lieutenant colonel, he evidently mistakes the crown and star on the cuff for two stars! 'Here young fellow,' says the major, 'don't you know a field officer when you see him?'

'Yes, I do,' says the colonel.

'Well, why the devil don't you salute, you damned young cub? What's your regiment?' says the major.

'I salute my seniors,' replies the boy quietly. The bleary eyes of the major fall on the fatal cuff. He gasps, turns and makes for the bar, there to fortify himself with another drink. We want to go there too and do so. We probably save the field officer from a still wetter night as he departs after our entry. This is a war for youngsters.

We are reduced to cadres and, later, even these are taken away.

While we select fortified positions for Chinese coolies to work on, under engineer supervision, all leave to England being stopped, I venture a request for four days' local recreation at the base. This is granted.

The activities of a huge army, such as was the British Army in France, operating in a friendly country, made it inevitable that from time to time civil offences should crop up for trial by military courts. It speaks volumes for the conduct of the men of the British armies of that period that so little purely civilian crime – such as murder and base and bestial offences – should have come before the military field courts.

The flight of the Portuguese led to some startling incidents, which were glossed over in the after-math of defeat. For instance, a British military motor driver was shot dead, his vehicle being commandeered, turned round and driven off by Portuguese who were petrified by their fear and demented by their danger.

On the other hand, a tragedy was enacted in the British area, which can only be accounted for by the war itself.

A British N.C.O. had been bullying some of his subordinates. As there appeared to be no way of dealing with the case there, aggrieved men decided to deal with the matter in their own way. As the essence of crime, from the criminal's point of view, is to leave no trace, they decided to get rid of their tormentor in the manner which they thought most suited to that purpose.

A Mill's bomb has a local but very violent explosive effect. They decided that the Mill's bomb should therefore be their agent. They caught their victim bending so to speak. Pulling out the pin from the bomb which held the lever in check and which, in its turn, ignited the charge which exploded after the lapse of some seconds, one of them – they had previously drawn lots for the job – pushed the bomb down the back of the N.C.O.'s trousers after which they made off at lightning speed to avoid the explosion.

Fortunately the poor man was isolated and entirely alone or others would have been killed – but he, ignorant till too late of what had happened, was, figuratively speaking, hoisted to glory by his own petard, for he, of course, became a battle casualty. There was no trace whatsoever left of this N.C.O. while, of course, there was no evidence available; but, from the legal point of view I much doubt if a charge of murder can be sustained without the production of some portion of the body for purposes of identification. This case still sends a cold chill down my spine when I think of it. There were so many bombs about and so many opportunities.

Some authors have been assailed for writing certain things they say they actually saw or had proof of. My own experience of war, which is a prolonged one, is that *anything* may happen in it, from the very highest kinds of chivalry and sacrifice to the very lowest form of barbaric debasement – whatever that may be.

I am ever so tired – weary – only another big battle, I think, will revive the spirit, unless Paris and Paris Plage do the trick.

I certainly see fun in Paris Plage. I loll about in the sun and take note of war life on the fringe, while I think of the past three years. I recall I have trained, or helped to train, seven new battalions, each of which has fought itself out of the Army List. Of these, one has been built up three times to the full again from nothing save a battle record, and all the others have 'come back,' twice before entirely disappearing from the order of battle. The total casualties sustained in the effort approximates seven thousand five hundred other ranks, and three hundred officers – mostly boys. And, I think, we are not yet out of the wood! I shake myself and seek solace in the dances and music! As I look at and join in with these boys and women young and old, I feel we are all half mad. Well we need be! I feel it is impossible for the good souls at home in sheltered seclusion to know to what lengths the mentality of the war generations has been strained. They cannot know the damage done, apart from battle casualties.

'Will Monsieur dance?' asks a pretty girl. 'Yes, Monsieur will dance' – anything to get out of the rut. We dance until 11 o'clock when the band goes off and the lights go out.

'No,' I say, 'I must go home; I'm tired' – '*Monsieur fatigué?*' she exclaims! At that moment an orderly appears from the town major's office and hands me an urgent letter. I open it. I can go home for four days if I like but I must get back at the end of that time as I am to form a new brigade which has to be in action within a month! I live again! The old vim has returned! Into the line again, I think, three new battalions once more, thank goodness I have a good staff! Home for four days . . . shall I ? . . . No, I can't. . . . I can't face the parting. Ten days gives a small period of forgetful oblivion, but four days – no– it would mean thinking of return on the moment of arrival – I can't! But it was good of the divisional commander to arrange it.

No – I shall return tomorrow and start building again – for the line – I look up, the girl is waiting!

'Oh! I'm busy,' I say. 'Here's twenty francs, go and play.' She trots off with a lad of twenty. On my way to my hotel I meet a doctor I know. He is staying the night at my hotel, so we sit up for a 'buck.'

'Tell me, doctor,' I say, 'can you account for this? An hour ago I was tired, mentally and physically, and I was also fed up. I then heard I had to go to the line again and raise a new brigade – the last one is bust up. My old vigour is now returned. I am O.K., as fit as a fiddle. Can you explain?'

'Yes,' he replies, 'you see an object in view, an objective in fact. You have a reserve. It was also tired. The drums have started, your reserves have pulled themselves together. You draw on them. You are temporarily right. You can carry on. Your internal effort has mastered your inertia brought on by strain. Your only hope is to go on being in the line until the end.' He then goes on to explain –

'All the world is like it,' he says, 'more or less. The war is responsible. It hits men like you most.' 'Thank you, doctor,' I say. 'Good night and good luck. I'm off to the line tomorrow.' 'You've done me good,' he says, 'can I come too?' 'Do you really want to?' I ask. 'Yes,' he says, 'I swore I never would go back, but I feel I must.' 'All right,' I say, 'shall we go and see your chief tomorrow?' 'Righto!' he replies.

We go to the line together once more.

# CHAPTER X

THE sluice gates are open. Life is not unpleasant as we idle in a farm on the water's edge near Saint-Omer, waiting for the arrival of the 'B' men who will form the new battalions. We boat on the flooded fields and go shopping in the Dutch style, for the whole country for miles around has been turned into a sea of released canal water which is to serve as a barrier between the Germans and the Channel ports, should there be a break through up north. It has taken over two weeks to get the waters sufficiently dispersed, while thousands of pounds worth of crops have been destroyed.

As I sit, after lunch, in the little garden, sunning myself, a car drives up. It has the G.H.Q. flag on the bonnet. Good heavens, I think, what on earth does it want here? It must have made a mistake!

An immaculately dressed young gentleman steps out and comes towards me. He salutes. 'What can I do for you?' I ask. 'My general sent me down

Sir, to see you about the 'B' men who will arrive tomorrow; he says he is afraid you will be disappointed——' I hold my hand up, as a sign for him to stop. 'Don't say any more, please,' I say 'I have heard that remark before. There are no bad soldiers, only bad colonels. What colonels are you sending me?' I ask.

'I don't know,' he replies.

'The usual, I suppose,' I say, 'fed-ups from the "pot-luck pool!" It won't do,' I add, shaking my head: 'the worse the man, the better the officer must be. Will you tell your general if I have good colonels, majors, adjutants, quartermasters and transport officers, and fair, but not soft doctors, the men can be made to do 'A' men's work?' He promises to give my message. Meanwhile transport arrives complete for three battalions. I look at it: it's good and its officers seem to know their work. Next day I ride out to meet the three battalions which are marching from a station not many miles off.

I spy two officers sitting on the road-side. On nearing them I see old Plunkett! My luck's in, I think. 'One good battalion at any rate,' I say to the staff officer who rides beside me.

Dear old Plunkett is the same as ever. He has had a bad time with his heart and had the greatest difficulty in getting them to let him come back to

France. After that he was to be sent to a soft job from the 'pool'; but, on hearing men were coming to us, he saw the commandant of the camp at the base and insisted on being sent up!

'You'll have to have a good weed out,' he says; 'many of the men are physically unfit, but many only fancy themselves ill; if you keep on combing out you will get a good brigade in the end.'

'What are your officers like?' I ask. 'Oh, some seem good, but I shall have to get rid of a lot,' he answers. 'What battalion have you got?' I ask. 'I don't think it has a number yet,' he answers; 'but it belongs to the Inniskilling Fusiliers.' 'Where are they?' I ask. 'Oh, they can't march yet,' he laughingly replies. 'They, and the other two battalions, the East Lancs and North Staffs, are strung out along the road for four miles – that's why I'm here! You'll have to weed out at once, get more, weed them out, and so on: there are plenty of quite fit men at the base: it's only a question of combing.'

I see the regimental doctors and tell them what I want. They comb out about fifty per cent. of the old fellows whom they consider beyond hope of physical redemption. After repeating this perform- ance with fresh drafts, we at length have three battalions and a trench-mortar battery which I consider will be capable of being mesmerised out of themselves. 'It is great to forget one is ill: it is fine to be fit,' became our slogan.

Within a very few days of the arrival of our veterans we proceed to Hazebrouck to be nearer the line and to carry out our musketry training on the ranges and be ready to hold a reserve line in order to receive the Germans on bayonets, should they break through near Strazeel!

'I suppose,' I say, to Plunkett, 'they think we shall be safe there, as we can't run away!'

The men are now pretty fit. They can march fairly well, and even run.

I receive an order from G.H.Q. which they tell me is to be read to the men. I am horrified at the wording of this order. It promises the 'B' men they will not be put into offensive action! 'Is not,' I ask, 'a local counter-attack offensive action, is not offence the soul of defence?' I put the order in my pocket and say nothing – for the time being. Later, I meet Plunkett. 'What about some sports for the men?' I ask. 'Good,' he replies. 'Will you run a brigade committee?' I ask. 'Certainly,' he says, 'I'll see the staff captain about it.'

The sports are a great success. The times are good. The team-races and inter-company events are excellent. All three battalions compete in one event, every man jack having to complete the course, for a prize. I am asked to give the prizes away.

I see my chance. 'I am glad,' I say, 'to see you all so happy. You have all done well in the sports, and have proved yourselves equal to 'A' men beyond doubt. Do you agree?' I ask. 'If so, say so!' (They all cheer violently). 'You have not had beer on payment because it was considered your health might suffer if you drank beer – I propose to provide you with beer as soon as it can be obtained' (loud cheers). 'The enemy is at our gates, are we down-hearted?' ('No', comes the deafening reply). 'Shall we give 'em hell if they have the bad luck to come in our way?' (loud cries of 'let 'em come'). 'Shall we ask to be 'A' men?' ('we are' comes the wanted reply). 'What is our war cry? Is it "steadily shoulder to shoulder?" If so, say so!' (loud cheers).

'We have done the trick,' I say to Plunkett. 'Now, let's have a scrap,' he replies. Going into the line near Strazeel, I offer £5 to the first men in each battalion to bring in a prisoner, and £1 for every other during the first tour. The German line is in a state of flux and isolated posts abound. It is said I should not offer money for prisoners; but I don't think there is anything wrong in so doing. Lord Wolseley gave a prize of £100 for the best time taken by the battalions hauling their boats over a cataract of the River Nile – I paid up £16, one battalion obtaining two prisoners and the remaining two one each.

It becomes my duty to go to division to command in the absence of the divisional commander, and while there I take part in the celebration of the outbreak of the war on August 4th. I stand near General Plumer and the Duchess of Sutherland, during the march past, after the service, and throw my memory back twenty years, almost to the very day, when I took the graceful lady in to dinner in the Lews as a mere boy. 'Time flies,' I say to the A.D.C., 'but the duchess does not alter!' First swing by the Artillery and then the youngsters of the other divisions, in the 2nd Army, while my old and bold – and now rejuvenated – bring up the rear. 'What's the matter with them, Sir?' I say to the army commander, who looks surprised at my remark. He has not noticed they are 'B' men on paper and 'A' men in the field!

We lunch at the Sauvage, at Cassel, in the same room from the windows of which I viewed the final stage of the Battle of Hazebrouck, while lunching, on my way up to reconnoitre, with fifty officers in trench kit, while the French transport lumbered through the narrow street outside. Modern war takes its twists and turns as surely as war ever has. On arrival back at headquarters I find a G.H.Q. car waiting, and in it sit two officers. They get out as I approach. 'May they see me alone?' they ask. We enter my office. The door is carefully shut.

One of the officers is on the staff, as I know by his cap, while the other is a general list man.

'Well,' I say, 'what can I do?'

'Have you a man called Lightlive in your brigade?' asks the staff officer.

'I don't know,' I reply, 'but I'll ask' . . . taking up the telephone receiver.

'Yes,' I say, after some conversation and delay. 'He wrote a letter to his wife,' says the staff officer, 'which Capt. Stickler here of the censor's department, opened. In it he tells his wife, if she is not satisfied with the money he gives her, she had better sit in the hotels and earn more, as she has a fortune in her face.' He pauses, and looks at me. 'Go on,' I say. 'The A.G.'s department considers this is a very serious and nasty case. Here is an officer, holding the King's commision, trying to prostitute his wife.' He looks at me again and pauses. 'Well?' I ask. 'Don't you think it is dreadful, Sir?' he asks. 'Are you sure it is his wife?' I answer. 'The letter is addressed to Mrs. Lightlive,' he says. 'Quite,' I reply, 'but that proves nothing! Anyway,' I ask, 'what's the censor for, morals or military matters? But what do you want me to do,' I add. 'Well, that's what we don't know exactly,' he replies, 'and we want your opinion both as his brigade and divisional commander.' 'I see,' I say. 'Well, first of all I should advise the A.G.'s department to learn about the national army and the times in which we are living; secondly, to get out of its mind that the censor is for morals; and thirdly, to find out, if it wants to, although I think it rather futile, if Lightlive is married. The army is no more moral than any other section of society. Why should it be? The divorce courts prove that. If Lightlive is not married, your case falls to the ground: if he is, even then I don't think you can interfere.' 'Will you find out for us?' he says. 'No, I won't,' I emphatically reply. 'Lightlive may be quite a good man in the field, and what he is in other places doesn't interest me in the slightest, outside France, provided he keeps himself fit! But if you like we'll ask him to dinner tonight. I have no idea what he's like, or if he eats his peas off a knife. I never recommend men for commissions now, unless I can see they are sahibs, without inserting on the form in the certificate, "in accordance with the standard at present in vogue!" Then *you* can ask him in the course of conversation, if he is married, though even then you won't have conclusive proof, as he may smell a rat and get off the track, saying "Yes" when he means "No," or "No" when he means "Yes;" which he has a perfect right to do, as you have no right to enquire into his private affairs. What say?'

Lightlive, astonished, almost amazed and somewhat alarmed, for all the little slips of the past loom up in front of him, no doubt, comes to dinner! He is smart in appearance, a good but quiet talker, when drawn out, and is aged about twenty-three. He is a subaltern, wears the Military Cross and is obviously a sahib. Of course, he has not the slightest idea why he has been asked to dinner! The wine goes round, the port and cigars arrive, and the coffee is almost finished. Will he never ask? I think, for even I am now curious! Suddenly the conversation turns on wives. 'Are you married?' the G.H.Q. man asks casually of Lightlive, whom I have purposely put next to him. 'No, thank God,' comes the instant and emphatic retort. I have the greatest difficulty in keeping a straight face. The conversation flags, interest seems to have disappeared. 'You will wonder, Lightlive,' I say, looking at the G.H.Q. Officer, 'why you were asked to come to dinner?' 'Well, Sir,' he replies, 'I was rather anxious.' 'I don't wonder,' I say. 'A bit of an ordeal I know. The truth is I had heard of you from G.H.Q.,' ('Hadn't I?' I say aside to his next-door neighbour, who nods, not knowing what on earth is coming next), 'and I wanted to see how you would do as intelligence officer for my brigade. Would you like the job?' 'Indeed Sir, I would,' Lightlive answers brightly. 'Well;' I reply, 'you can have it.' 'May I ask one question, Sir?' asks Lightlive. 'Certainly.'

'How on earth did G.H.Q. get hold of my name?' he asks. 'Ah,' I laughingly answer, 'I can't tell you that, ask Knowall there!' Knowall merely remarks: 'We heard you were a thruster,' but he has one in for me as he slyly looks at me and says: 'And we know you like thrusters, General, don't you?'

Lightlive departs a much pleased and puzzled man. We sit on and talk – Knowall reverts to 'shop,' 'You know, General, you said you inserted words about "the standard in vogue" in your recommendations for commissions. I am interested, from the A.G.'s point of view, as to what effect that would have on a charge under Section 16, scandalous conduct, etc., of a *gentleman*?' 'I don't know in a point of law,' I say; 'but I had one case when a youngster was tried under Section 16, when he set up a defence that he never asked to be made an officer and never claimed to be a gentleman! I was, at the time, recommending several miners per week, by order, for commissions. Excellent N.C.O's no doubt, but impossible as officers. I was very sorry for them all, and I can't help feeling that that source would have been best left untapped.'

Soon Plunkett's time arrives for more blood and action. We advance our line and the valiant warrior earns a second bar to his D.S.O., the veterans of the brigade behaving as the stalwarts that they are.

Theirs is a veritable triumph of mind over matter, a true exposition of the command: 'Man, cure thyself.' A few months ago they were lounging about the bases and labour companies, saying they had 'done their bit.' Some are veterans of Mons, others the first to come up of the new army, while a few have been territorials for years. Never was there such age with honour, never such ripe experience. A proper system of training and saving would have equalised the working efficiency of the divisions (some of which were always mediocre, others always good – the result of chance appointments to command) and conserved the man-power for the last.

'What good is it,' I write, 'to comb out England to the bone, and let the dregs and so-called rubbish rot: there are no rubbishy soldiers.' I acquire a famous baritone singer, a territorial veteran of the cavalry, as orderly officer, who sings to the men in billets and to me in shellholes, and eventually manages the transport. Great is he, greater his voice.

A chance of leave appears and I go home. Cupid is running riot in London. In our hotel are three couples, the men are known to me, the girls self-conscious. 'Mum's the word,' I get from all, and 'mum' the word remains. It will take some time, I think, as I look at their daring intrigues, for

English decorum to settle down after the last shot is fired!

My leave is temporarily darkened by a series of sad events. I visit two relatives who are sisters. They live together, one has two sons serving, both fresh from school in 1914; the other, one of similar age. These are their all – their husbands being dead. At 9 a.m., a death telegram arrives, at noon is brought another, while at 6 p.m., the final message announcing the death in action of the third boy is received. As I look on at this tragedy my mind expands! . . . 'Ghastly,' I almost shout – 'What can be done? Nothing *yet* – save win!'

I return to joy! The parting is not so trying. Why? The enemy is on the run. The avalanche has melted. Naught now remains, save to gather up the harvest!

My troubles over colonels have been fierce. The 'pot-luck pool' has sent its luck all right; but it has been of the tiresome sort. Some desired not to fight, others said their veterans were unable to. To one I was a butcher! To another – mad! and consequently the procession back to 'pot-luck' was well sustained. But now I am saved, for Andrews, limping, yet still the old fire-eating Andrews, has put his foot in France. Finding out our whereabouts he asks for a few days' leave to Paris, but comes to

Bailleul in the wrong train! He commands the East Lancs and finishes the war in the van.

The North Staffords are in trouble; the same old cause – colonels! Our luck is in – I find an Irish soldier in the line commanding a hundred men. 'Your history? Can I have it?' I ask him in a shell-hole. 'His name? O'Connor, late company sergeant major of the Irish Guards, and now a captain of the Munsters,' he replies. 'Do you know a fellow called O'Connor?' I ask at lunch. 'Yes, I think he's good,' the staff captain answers. 'Post him to command the North Staffs,' I say. He transforms the battalion and electrifies the men in under a week – in the nick of time.

We head for Houplines and the re-crossing of the Lys. What a difference to five months ago, I think, when Amery-Parkes and Campbell sold themselves dearly in their great endeavour to dam the flowing tide. We race the 'A' Division on our left – 'the old 'uns' win, thanks largely to their own pluck and the scouting efforts of Muirhead, brigade major, for which he obtains a bar to his M.C.

In Houplines we meet gas in vast quantities, and Lamb – Mutton we call him – signalling officer and mess president, who once dared to mix claret with port, to make the latter go further, and was foolish enough to think Muirhead of Magdalen wouldn't notice it – gulps too much and goes down. It looks as if we are at close quarters here. Will the Boche try a cut out? All hands to the rifles is the order. Knowles' servant, Richardson, who long ago thought he was at the base for good, has come to the line without his rifle! 'I'm C.2' he almost cries, when asked why he has not got his gun. 'That won't save you,' acidly remarks the brigade major, 'a rifle might!' Cold comfort for a C.2 man!

The casualties are pretty heavy for the class of warfare; but hidden machine guns left with the rearguard take no account of difference in medical category. The North Staffs lose twelve officers one day.

Still the old and the bold march on. We enter Roubaix, the great industrial town. The population, recently liberated, go mad while the German rearguards are not yet clear of the eastern suburbs. The veterans come into their own.

'This is better than the base, boys,' shouts one stalwart to his pal in front. 'This is what we got in '14 when we arrived,' says another. 'It's a damned long way to Roubaix, but my heart's right there,' sings a third, as a factory girl throws him a bouquet which he catches.

And then comes tragedy once more. The war is not yet over; it is October, and there is to be tragedy still and even after.

These men who laugh, and chaff and sing, stand

on parade later for inspection. They know it not, but they are standing over the very jaws of death. Under their feet is a huge charge of explosives, timed to go off shortly.

There is a terrific roar, every window for hundreds of yards round is broken, houses shake, walls collapse. A dozen odd valiant warriors are blown to their long rest, a few days before peace arrives. Some bits are picked up and buried. As I follow the *cortège* the bands drum out the Dead March on their way to the little French cemetery.

Is this a gentle reminder that we are not yet out of the wood?

We move forward to the River Scheldt at Pecq. Poor Pecq, unscathed until November, 1918, it is demolished in a day. The shelling is considerable. A rearguard disputes the passage of the canalised river. An attack on a large scale is planned, which necessitates the forcing of the river and an advance over open country to the plateau beyond. For this enterprise the East Lancs, Staffords and 'Skins' are specially put back into the line out of their turn. My memory flashes back to the G.H.Q. 'no offensive' order. What, had I published it?

Temporary bridges are thrown across the river at night. Patrols of 'old men' are pushed out across the causeways. The bird is beginning to fly, so come back the reports. '*Allez, Allez*' commands Andrews,

'Follow me,' shouts O'Connor. 'Damn it, I'm out of it,' says Plunkett. The old and bold lead the whole Army! Two Germans are bayoneted in a crater while the rest of the post surrender. 'Who are these Herculean blood-men from the North Midlands, Lancashire, and Ireland?' ask the astonished prisoners? 'We were told,' they say, 'that the cripples of England were opposite us, but if these are your cripples, what of the rest?' But Plunkett is not out of it for long. The front expands, he takes his place, mounted, as was his own colonel at Mons, when he was sergeant major, four years and three months ago!

'Mercy, mercy,' shouts an German ex-waiter on the left, as he sees the cold steel of a North Staffordshire potter quivering above his head, for he has been felled by a rifle butt swung by a Wolverhampton striker of past four-and-forty years. 'Mercy be damned,' shouts the potter, whose blood is up, as he thrusts to the wind pipe in the most up-to-date manner.

The time is short. It is now 11 a.m., on 8th November.

The word goes round, for an order has been received for instant promulgation: 'If any bearer of a white flag of truce is seen to approach our lines,' the order runs, 'he is to be conveyed at once, blindfolded, to the nearest headquarters.' The East

A WRECKED BRIDGE OVER THE RIVER SCHELDT, CROSSED BY 'THE BOYS OF THE OLD BRIGADE' ON THE NIGHT OF NOVEMBER 7TH-8TH, 1918

Lancs and North Staffs capture a field gun. A whole Belgian village is gassed and destroyed, the inhabitants being poisoned, by the unavoidable action of our gunners. The time runs on. A machine gunner unhorses a Uhlan of the rearguard. 'My gum,' says one old soldier of the pre-war type, 'I haven't seen one of those ——s since that night after Cateau in '14!'

The sands are running out.

I go to see Andrews who is throwing out outposts for the night. 'You haven't seen a flag of truce yet?' I chaffingly ask. 'We don't see flags of truce,' he replies. 'God help any man carrying a flag of truce who comes near us!'

The fatal message arrives. Plunkett, Andrews, O'Connor – all want to attack. I stop them. Not a life is to be thrown away, I say.

We are squeezed out of the line. All is quiet.

That night we dine with Belgian nobility, in whose château we sleep. We provide the food, since they have none, while the *grand seigneur* departs to the woods to dig up some priceless old wine, which has lain hidden under the leaves and mould for over four long years. 'The family silver plate is in the pond,' he says, 'please excuse us.'

'*A la santé, mon Général,*' he smilingly says, '*à l'armée Britannique, aux hommes magnifiques,*' he adds as he lifts his glass – 'That's the old and the bold he means,' I say.

The hour strikes eleven on the eleventh day of the eleventh month.

Let us not forget it.

Let us see where our duty lies.

# CHAPTER XI

## AFTER THE STORM

THE serving soldier naturally looks on war, its preparation, and its conduct as his task in life. He cannot and must not look outside his narrow blinkers. He believes in his power of destruction as do his possible adversaries. There the matter ends.

It is for others to lead the way down the avenue of sanity. We can only point. I can only judge the military minds of soldiers by my own mind, when I was serving, and before I began to study the blessings of peace. Here is an instance of my own narrow-minded mentality in 1918. Sir William Birdwood issued orders that the city of Lille was not to be bombarded. I received the orders with mixed feelings. 'But,' I said, 'there are Germans inside, what of them, are they to escape?' I was bent on destruction.

Only those men who actually march back from the battle line on 11th November, 1918, can ever know or realise the mixed feelings then in the hearts of combatants. We are dazed. When Germans, Frenchmen, Belgians, and Britishers rise and stretch at 11 a.m., in the presence of each other, with an inner feeling of insecurity, lest some one may 'do the dirty,' and be tempted to fire off a parting shot, they are dazed – for no fighting man worth his salt desired at that moment to do anything but forget the past and forge the future.

All the world over, where men and women congregated in large numbers they went mad. Not so the fighting men fresh from the line, dumped down in the liberated areas, where children beg for bread and grown-ups thank God for delivery.

While the stay-at-homes of victorious countries are dancing, and drinking in the capitals of Europe, and patting themselves on the back because they have won the war, Andrews, the valiant Andrews, thruster, fighter and man of action, is issuing his remaining mess stores personally to little children who have never seen or cannot remember a tin of fruit or known a Christmas party.

We march back to Croix.

Many of the men wear garlands, the gifts of grateful people to old warriors no longer in the first flush of youth, who have stuck it to the end, while some carry joy banners, seized as souvenirs from the cottage tops of hamlets.

As we cross the right Pecq causeway, over which

British soldiers crawled at the alert at midnight, three days ago, we skirt the crater. At the bottom lie the two dead steel-helmeted Germans still unburied, while ten yards off in a neat grave on the roadside with rough cross and freshly writ inscription, lie the mortal remains of the last British soldier of the 119th Infantry Brigade to be killed in 'the war, to end war.'

We read the inscription: 'He died for his country.' 'What about the two blokes in the hole?' asks Andrews lightly, 'I suppose they did too? 'Yes,' I reply, 'but unfortunately for them, they were on the wrong side!'

'Wasn't it a pity,' says my orderly officer, standing beside me, 'that that poor fellow of ours had to go west at the very end? I suppose it wasn't possible to call a halt before?' 'Pressure must be continued to the very end in war, otherwise the vanquished take advantage,' I tell him. 'It is just like industrial magnates and work-people continually at war with each other, not caring a hang about the suffering caused to others and the country.'

We pass through Pecq. 'Poor old Pecq,' says Andrews, looking at the ruined houses, 'fancy getting that in the last week of the war! What had it done to deserve it?' 'Nothing,' I reply; 'what had Kennedy done?'

At Croix is a considerable British population

employed in the Holden works. I go to see Mr. Guthrie, the senior British resident.

'Very glad to see you at last,' he says to me, as I sit with him in the board room of the works, 'we had a bad time for four years.'

'Did they ill-treat you?' I ask. 'They were pretty rough,' is his reply. 'The Crown Prince stayed here in this house several times, with a few of his staff. When they came I hid my young daughters in the attic. I wasn't taking any chances. Twice they swore I was hiding them – I said they were away – some one had told them I had girls of my own.'

'What about the food?' I ask. 'Oh we just managed to exist on vegetables and the like. The French workers were in a terrible state. You notice when you walk about in the streets you will see no dogs or cats – they were all eaten.'

'I hope my brigade won't be in your way, in your works?' I ask. 'It is wonderful having them all under one roof.' 'I wish we had the machinery under the roof instead of your men, welcome though they be,' he says: 'they stripped every bit of machinery, steel, iron or other useful commodity we possessed, and took it back to Germany.'

'When the British Army gets to the Rhine, do you think the Germans will have such a bad time as we had?' he asks. 'I'm sure they won't, 'I reply. 'First of all the war is over, and most people are tired of hating: secondly, our system is different to the German system, although we are like them in many other respects. The British Tommy is a wonderful fellow in strange countries, and I'll be bound in a couple of years or so – if we are to stay on – the Germans will actually love him, he is such a gentleman.'

Meanwhile Christmas Day arrives – the birthday of the Prince of Peace and lover of children. The veterans and their officers entertain the French youngsters within their areas. We all, also, attend a special Christmas pantomime for the children, in the Roubaix Theatre, which we rent for the day. Colonel Plunkett, of Mons and Bourlon, treble D.S.O., M.C., D.C.M., marches at the head of three hundred children, while his band plays the *Marseillaise*, and his officers and N.C.O.'s act as ushers and help on the toddlers.

Andrews and O'Connor do the same. And what of Cologne? The British mentality is predominatingly uniform. The children of all nations, belligerents and neutrals alike, have been the innocent victims of a great misfortune! They did not make the war, they merely suffered and lost. So thinks a manly parson at Cologne, with the result that the German children share in the joys of Christmas, as guests of British soldiers, on the birthday of the Prince of Peace.

I journey to Brussels and Cologne – but before

departure I talk seriously with my colonels. 'The men have evidently gone woman-mad,' I say. 'The venereal sick-rate is mounting. Many women must be diseased. I hear the Germans let the diseased women out of prison the day we arrived. It was an offence for a French woman to give a German soldier venereal, for which she was locked up, for the protection of the soldiers of course! As the army is now returning to England by degrees it is essential that, so far as is possible, we protect the women at home by returning their men clean. You must lecture your men on the subject and provide every convenient and reliable means of protection and sterilisation. I will see the mayor about the detection of the women and their treatment and segregation.'

At Brussels is an orgy of vice in which many British soldiers join.

The high-class prostitutes of the German Army are taken over by the officers of the allied forces – yet – only one short month ago, nothing was too bad for a German, nothing too good for ourselves! I see a British corps commander, lost in the whirl of post-battle gaiety, accosted by a woman of easy virtue, to his great annoyance, in the lift of his hotel. Her chief claim to his attention, according to her views, is that she was the war-time mistress of a German general!

In the halls and dining-rooms, these ladies line up as they did in the days of German occupation. The women are the same, only the men and their uniforms are different, while the constant procession of couples to bedrooms aloft is as sustained and regular as in the days of German domination! And what of Cologne? There the servant girls in hotels, half starved, lacking the ordinary necessaries of life, and even unused to simple crusts, pick up the crumbs which fall from their masters' tables and sell their bodies for half loaves of bread, in order that they may take to the aged and young in their homes the staff of life, that commodity akin to manna.

Realising the trials and dangers of demobilisation, I tighten up the discipline, arrive at a proper understanding with those who await their turn to cast off the war uniform, and provide counter attractions, so far as is possible, in order to avert the chaos which I feel sure will be the inevitable sequel to disappointment and disillusionment: for soldiers are but human and all cannot be demobilised at once. Elsewhere impatient men burn their camps, and huts, assault their officers, imprison their generals, and the staffs, and hold up demobilisation itself – the very thing they wish to speed up – by their mutinous conduct and the destruction of the demobilisation papers. In one instance a British division is marched to Calais from Flanders, to restore order.

The majority of the men are savage for freedom. Tactful handling of problems is required, and when this is the rule the British soldier is, as usual, sensible.

Mutiny is the invariable outcome of official incompetence, and when mutineers are punished, as must always be the case – for no mutiny can be condoned – responsible senior officers should invariably share a similar fate. This was not done in 1919.

At last I receive orders to proceed to England to report at the War Office.

I drive to 'Wipers' to see the ruins. I walk over the battlefields of Thiepval, Bourlon, Ervillers, Mory, the Lys and the Somme, for the last time.

The silence in these places in uncanny – as I pass over the sacred spots sanctified for ever to the sacrifices and valour of such men as George Gaffikin, Campbell, Kennedy, Morgan, Andrews, Amery-Parkes, and Gough, my soul seems to rebel within me. I think of the wasters who avoided military service 'for conscience sake'; or who sought security at home doing their bit in uniform – and yet well out of it all. 'Good heavens,' I say to my companion, as I stand on the spot where my orderly killed the German with the Very light, 'I can't stand this, let us to Boulogne and Blighty, to forget – every inch of this ground hides a tragedy.' 'I think,' he wisely remarks, 'Boulogne and almost every other place in Europe has and hides as many tragedies.'

Arriving at our hotel at Boulogne to spend the night, while at coffee in the lounge, after dinner, my eyes fall on Margot – the pretty waitress who had waited on the thousands of British officers during the past four years and nine months. She is crying. She is very upset. We call her over. She is very reticent, – but at last, breaking down completely, she unburdens her heart. Her trouble is simple. She has loved and been loved by many British officers during the hectic days – we guessed as much. Money has come easily. Excitement triumphed over remorse. She kept going while she supported an aged mother. Then she really fell in love with a good-looking young British officer, the son of a noble house, who – having slept with her on many occasions – promised to marry her. He had just jilted her. Hence the tears, the remorse, the utter disillusionment. The glamour, excitement and prosperity of war have disappeared – only utter disappointment remains for this poor girl.

Next morning as we enter the lounge after breakfast there is no Margot. She has joined the millions of other war victims. Demented, prostrate with anguish, frightened of the future, alone, forgotten, ignored, and perhaps wounded in pride – with British officers leaving France daily in large numbers, and her real lover ignoring her frantic appeals – she blew out her brains with a German pistol once given her by a colonel. 'I told you Boulogne has its war tragedies as well as the battlefields,' remarks my companion.

And then I pass out of the Great War and as I stand on the leave boat for the last time, looking at Boulogne, I say to a companion who is beside me, 'It may be for ever, in so far as this uniform is concerned, but there is a scar – unseen to any – slashed across my soul which will be with me to the end.' Am I the only man, at this moment, who feels this?

Shortly after I arrive home I go to see Madge who now has a little son a year old. I have not seen the child before, as his mother has been in the country. Madge is delighted to see me.

'How like his father!' I say, as I pick him up.

'I'm so glad you think so!' she says, looking adoringly at the child, who never saw his father, and whom his father never saw.

'May Ogden is coming to see you,' she says, 'I asked her to tea. She wants to see you so much, and you might be able to help about her pension; she thinks she should have a little more money for her daughter Grace's education; the girl is at an important age.'

'I haven't seen her since that awful day we broke the news to her at Victoria – I'm afraid there wasn't much break about it, it was so abrupt. How is she?' I say.

'Oh she's splendid! As splendid as you men used to be, and she and I are great friends,' says Madge.

'Frank,' says Madge, 'I never thought you'd get through the hellish ———' 'Mrs. Ogden,' announces the maid, which puts an end to our conversation.

The war widow is still a girl, despite her loss. I promise to see Sir James Craig at the Ministry of Pensions about her grant. Madge does most of the talking as she reads all the papers and sees things from a broad angle, while I am out of touch with England.

'I'm not going to have my Tim killed in another war, like his brave Daddy, am I?' says Madge, taking the child on her lap.

'I wish I could think there will never be another war,' says Mrs. Ogden, placing her hand on Grace's head. 'I don't dare to think of Grace losing her husband, perhaps after I'm gone; but wars seem to be inevitable, don't they?' she asks.

'Not in the least,' says emphatic and positive Madge. 'They are a stupid and man-made invention, without a single redeeming feature,' she went on to say, 'and if we women can't abolish war ourselves we shall deserve the consequences. We must get at and conquer the causes which create the effect.'

'What do you think, General?' asks Mrs. Ogden.

'There never need be another war,' I say, 'if we all play the game!'

'It is the last resource of fools!' says Madge.

Ten years pass by.

Madge and I are dining quietly at Hatchett's.

'I like to dine here occasionally,' she says; 'it reminds me of pre-war days with you and Tim.'

'How are those wonderful colonels of yours you used to talk about?' she asks.

'You meant Plunkett, Andrews and Benzie?' I say.

'Yes,' she replies.

'The after-effect of war has hit them all,' I say. 'Plunkett was invalided out, a total wreck some years after the Armistice. Bourlon did him in. Andrews became mentally deranged for a time, in France, directly after the war finished – he snapped – but getting better went to Russia and was captured by the Bolos and spent months in a gaol. He is dead. Benzie I saw not long ago, looking very ill: he returned to Ceylon but was invalided for good. There are thousands of men in Europe today suffering from the effects of war, who can never hope to get better and whose sufferings are not known. They are the men who wouldn't go sick, because it was not the thing to do.'

'You mean,' she says, 'they belong to the legion

who dazzled us with their valour and staggered us with their daring deeds?'

'Yes,' I reply.

'Well,' she says, 'all is not gold that glitters!'

There must never be another grand parade.

It isn't worth it!

It is simply a question of S.O.S.!

The great war was the S.O.S. danger signal to civilization. If we ignore that S.O.S. and the lessons of the war, civilization is doomed.

# EPILOGUE

# EPILOGUE

It was in the year 2119 that there assembled in London, at the invitation of the King of England, people from all parts of the earth, to celebrate the two hundredth anniversary of the foundation of the League of Nations.

On this occasion the people of the world, through their representatives, offered up their thanks to Almighty God, in Westminster Abbey, close to the tomb of the Unknown Warrior, for bountiful mercies and abundant prosperity which had been vouchsafed to them through the instrumentality of common sense and the sacrifices of mankind during the World War.

London had been chosen as the venue for this great historic gathering because it was there that in the year 1930 a constructive advance into the realm of disarmament and co-operation had been made at an international conference, held to further the advent of real peace.

A jamboree of boy scouts from all the world over was also being held concurrently with the League of Nations celebrations, to honour the two hundred and twenty first anniversary of the founding of the movement by the great soldier-thinker, Lord Baden-Powell; for great also had been the contribution of the Scouts and Guides to the Peace of the World.

On August 4th, 2119 (the two hundred and fifth anniversary of the outbreak of the Great War) a scoutmaster was conducting a party of boy scouts through the Museum of Military Antiquities. 'This building in which you now are,' said the scoutmaster, 'was at one time what was known as the War Office. From here the land victory was directed which eventually and entirely altered the mentality of man. After the so-called victory in the field, it began to dawn on the rulers of the world, through force of public opinion, that the machinery of world government had not kept pace with the growth of world economic and industrial development. The League of Nations with its world-controls was the result.'

They passed on in silence, gazing wonderingly at curious lethal weapons, and armoured protection of all kinds, deadly gasses in sealed jars, flame projectors, containers, and every imaginable kind of device which man, aided by science, could invent for the purpose of wholesale destruction of life, morality and property. They reached a picture gallery. 'In this chamber,' said the scoutmaster, 'propaganda,

G.O.C. AND STAFF, 119TH INFANTRY BRIGADE, 11TH NOVEMBER, 1918

forged passports, and the like, secret ciphers, faked dossiers and all kinds of unscrupulous subterfuges for the conduct of war were devised.'

'Please Sir,' asked a small boy, 'what is a passport?'

'Well,' answered the master, 'it is difficult to explain; but in days of old when people wished to travel from one country to another, in peace time as well as war, they had to get permission on a passport to do so, both from their own country and the country they wished to visit.'

'But why was that necessary?' interrupted the youthful enquirer.

'Because people were suspicious of each other,' answered the master; 'but,' he went on, 'on our way out we will go to the curious customs room and see some old official passports, both of the genuine and forged variety. Governments used both.'

They walked on in silence.

'There,' said the master, pointing to the wall, 'you see some great British soldiers; the Duke of Cambridge, Wolseley, Roberts, Kitchener, Wilson, Haig and Robertson. They were great Britishers. Read what is written under Robertson's picture, 'I suggest that every man and woman should energetically support all efforts made for devising some more sensible and humane way of composing international difficulties, than the destructive and futile methods upon which reliance has hitherto been placed.'

'His utterances carried great weight in his day, and to him we owe much.'

'How funny it all seems that they should want to destroy to get on!' said the same small boy.

'Not according to their times,' said the master, 'they knew no better; only Robertson became inspired to spread the new gospel – the other Field Marshals died before the time, and some had not his war training and experience behind the scenes.'

'What made the people change?' asked the young enquirer.

'I think,' replied the master, 'they woke up to the appalling price they had to pay in blood, morality, and treasure for their victory. The men and women and mere boys and girls, gave of their very best during the great war. Their chivalry, courage and fortitude were unbounded. This was not confined to one side only; the wasted splendour all over the world was colossal. Then someone, H. G. Wells I think, said: 'The war of 1914 – 18 was to be the war to end war,' and many men died really believing that to be so. It is well it was so, because, after the survivors had time to think the matter over, they did not forget their responsibilities. They remembered the million dead of the British Empire, to say nothing of the widows and orphans, the maimed, the gassed and the crippled. Then they began to count the total World War loss of some ten million dead alone. Nobody can ever know what we of the Empire owe to the million British men and women who died to give us our present-day peaceful comfort and prosperity.'

'It behoves us to carry on their torch,' said a big boy, 'to make the British Empire worthy of them.'

'That is so,' replied the leader: 'we will go to see the statue of Nurse Cavell before we go back; on it you will see what she said just prior to her military execution in Brussels, during the Great War.'

'What did she say?' asked the same inquisitive small boy.

'She said: "Patriotism is not enough, I must have no hatred or bitterness for anyone,"' replied the master. 'But let us go in here before we leave – we may find something to interest us about our ancestors.'

'What room is this?' asked a boy who had hitherto been silent.

'It is what they call the Hall of Platitudes and Broken Promises,' replied the leader. 'Formerly it was the room in which the British Secretary of State for War presided over the Army Council. They did their very best for their country; but they too were on the wrong track altogether. Look what they used to go by. Up there you see an ancient shibboleth, which only the Great War exposed; "To ensure Peace, prepare for War" That platitude

251

was inscribed over the gate of one of their great arsenals. Over there is another misunderstanding behind which they sheltered: "Human nature never changes." Both those slogans when repeated parrot-like over and over again, became very dangerous beliefs. The first was only true to a limited extent. It was like two big bullies at school, of equal weight and height. Their strength made them fearful of each other, and they did not fight for a long time. Then, one of them, seeing his chance, took the other unawares. The result was of course that although one had taken a mean advantage of the other and consequently looked like knocking the other out at first, he didn't – as his opponent managed to stop the quick decision. Both fought on for a very long time and both were, eventually, carried off to hospital.'

'What about human nature never changing?' asked the small boy, who had been asking his leader such intelligent questions.

'Oh,' replied the leader, 'there again they made use of a half truth because it suited them. What they didn't realise was that as evolution goes on all the time, so our habits change despite the fact that human nature is always inclined to be cruel. Take those poor people who suffered so much during the Great War: they were evolving and their habits were changing. A hundred years before the Great

War their ancestors used to carry swords at all times, and fight duels. At last it became bad form to fight duels; so they went to the law courts instead, and as swords went out of fashion, sword makers went broke, for a time; but the workmen who made the swords turned their hands to other steel work and artistic designs. After the Great War it became bad form for nations to fight; so they too began to go to the law courts and arbitration tribunals for redress, as they found it very much cheaper and safer. Eventually, owing to this, the world demand for armaments ceased in the same way as the demand for swords had ceased, and now we come to our own process of evolution. Look out of that window and you will see the Ministry of Law and Order. That building used to be the Admiralty. There, during the great struggle of two hundred years ago, the great Lord Fisher, a sailor of repute, locked himself in his office and refused to speak to his chief, the great Winston Churchill, because, although they both wanted badly to save their country, they disagreed as to how it should be saved. Nothing like that can happen now, as the Ministry of Law and Order co-ordinates the active police work in conjunction with the greater Department of World Law and Order at the League of Nations at Geneva, to which it is subordinate in matters of world policy.'

'I see,' said the boy.

'Let us go, it is lunch time,' said the good British scoutmaster, 'for we can still eat beef steak as our great ancestors did.'

As they walked down the impressive marble stairs of the Museum of Military Antiquities, and turned to the right to pass through the imposing exit which leads to Whitehall, another small boy asked his master: 'What is that wax figure at the door?'

'That,' he replied, 'is the exact effigy of the last War Office hall porter, saluting members of the last Army Council, on their way to lunch at "the Senior" for the last time, prior to their abolition to give place to the Ministry of Law and Order.'

'What was the Senior?' asked the inquisitive small one.

'It was a place,' came the slowly considered reply, 'where old sailors and soldiers used to congregate to read newspapers, eat, sleep and say the country was going to the dogs.'

'But did it really go to the dogs? What a funny expression to use,' said the boy.

'Oh, dear no, it didn't, it was merely a figure of speech, a sign of evolution. The ancestors of those old warriors used to say funny things like "Zounds and Gadzooks." We shall appear just as funny two hundred years hence to our descendants.'

Lightning Source UK Ltd.
Milton Keynes UK
UKOW06f0132280515

252438UK00008B/118/P